HOW TO READ A PLAY

HOW TO READ A PLAY

Ronald Hayman

GROVE PRESS, INC.
NEW YORK

FOR JULIET
who helps
more than she realizes

First Edition 1977
Second Printing 1978
ISBN: 0-394-17022-9
Grove Press ISBN: 0-8021-4097-1
Library of Congress Catalog Card
Number: 77-002455

Manufactured in the United States
of America

Distributed by Random House, Inc.,
New York

GROVE PRESS, INC.,
196 West Houston Street,
New York, N.Y. 10014

Contents

Acknowledgements

Acknowledgements and thanks are due to the following for permission to quote from published works:

Faber & Faber Ltd and New Directions, New York, for an extract by Ezra Pound in William Carlos Williams's *Paterson*; Oxford University Press for extracts from Anton Chekhov's *Three Sisters* and *The Cherry Orchard*, in *The Oxford Chekhov*, translated and edited by Ronald Hingley; Secker & Warburg Ltd and The Viking Press for an extract from *Death of a Salesman*, printed in *Collected Plays* by Arthur Miller © 1949, renewed 1977 by Arthur Miller; Edward Albee, Jonathan Cape Ltd and Coward, McCann & Geoghegan Inc, for an extract from *Zoo Story* in *Zoo Story and Other Plays*; ACTAC (Theatrical & Cinematic) Ltd for extracts from a statement by Harold Pinter, first appearing as 'Between the Lines' in *The Sunday Times*, 4 March 1962, and revised in *The New British Drama*, Grove Press, 1964; Secker & Warburg Ltd for an extract from August Strindberg's *The Father*, translated by Michael Meyer; Eyre Methuen for extracts from Bertolt Brecht's *Life of Galileo* and *The Good Person of Szechwan*, translated by Marsh and Brooks and John Willett respectively, © 1955 by Suhrkamp Verlag Berlin, and © D. Vesey 1960 and John Willett 1962 respectively, and for extracts from Harold Pinter's *The Caretaker* and *The Birthday Party*; International Copyright Bureau Ltd for an extract from Nikolai Gogol's *The Government Inspector*, translated by Marsh and Brooks; Hart-Davis MacGibbon Ltd for an extract from Henrik Ibsen's *Hedda Gabler*, translated by Michael Meyer; J. M. Dent and Sons Ltd for an extract from Henrik Ibsen's *Rosmersholm,* translated by R. Farquharson Sharp in the Everyman's Library series; Calder & Boyars Ltd for an extract from Eugène Ionesco's *The Killer*, in *Plays Volume III*, and an extract by Samuel Beckett in *International Theatre Annual No. 1*; Faber & Faber Ltd for an extract reprinted from T. S. Eliot's *Four Quartets*, and with Grove Press, extracts, reprinted by permission from Samuel Beckett's *Waiting for Godot*; Granada Publishing Ltd for an extract by Peter Brook in *The Empty Space* published by MacGibbon & Kee Ltd; The Society of Authors on behalf of the Bernard Shaw Estate for an extract from George Bernard Shaw's *Man & Superman*.

Preface

A great many people derive a great deal of pleasure from reading plays. Would that pleasure be increased by an increase in their awareness of what they are doing? A script can be read casually, like a novel, mainly for the sake of the story, or it can be read, more like a code or a musical score, as a scenario for a series of theatrical impacts which can be achieved only in a public performance. Are we imagining actors moving on a stage or characters moving in a room? Do we even ask ourselves this question?

If you want to avoid self-consciousness about what you are doing when you read a script, do not read this book, which is written in the belief that the play comes more vividly to life in your mind if you are more alert to the technical problems the director and the actors have in bringing the words to theatrical life and to the psychological process of translating printed dialogue and stage directions into mental action.

The well-trained actor has learned how to respond to a script not just intellectually and emotionally: he may feel physically involved in the tugs and rhythms of the action. The director reads a script with one eye on the problem of how the words can be fleshed into three-dimensional life. Not that the reader needs two or three years of training at a drama school before he can expect to get the most out of a script when he settles into his armchair, but he can, I believe, develop his talent for forming vivid impressions of theatrical action. The intention behind this book is to help.

How should we read stage directions? How can we imagine the theatrical impact of a sound effect? And of a silence? What about the effect of colours, costumes, groupings, relative positions on the stage? Aren't characters sometimes saying something quite different from what their words are saying? What about the momentum an action can generate? Why is farce so much more amusing on the stage than on the page? These are some of the questions I try to answer in a book designed to contain as much practical help as I can give not just to the student and the specialist but to everyone for whom the word theatre is not merely the name of the building they go to when they can afford to buy tickets.

                                    I didn't
say it wuz! ! henjoyable readin.
I sd/ the guy had done some honest
work devilupping his theatre technique

―――――――――――――

That don't necess/y mean making
reading matter @ all.

                        Ezra Pound
Letter to William Carlos Williams

I

The reader and the medium

What is a play? – The set and the atmosphere – The use of space –
The play as a series of impacts – Stage directions about action

What is a play?

We all think we know what a play is, but no one has ever suc-
ceeded in defining it. A novel or a poem is neither more nor less
than the words it consists of, but a script is obviously less than a
play, while a production is obviously more. So how do we locate
its limits? Is it like a chemical substance which can never be
isolated, existing only in combination with other substances?

Reading a script can be all the more enjoyable if we remember
that it wasn't intended for reading. We see words; we imagine
sounds and pictures. When we go to the theatre, we hear words
and sounds, but we see people and backgrounds; when we read,
we use our eyes on the element that is invisible in performance.
During Shakespeare's lifetime, it was natural to talk of *hearing*
a play. 'We'll hear a play tomorrow,' promises Hamlet. 'Will the
King hear this piece of work?' Today, we always talk of *seeing* a
play, putting the emphasis on the action that is visible.

When we read a play or a novel, we cannot take in more than
one impression at a time. As our eyes move laterally across the
printed lines, our brain receives each impact separately. The
information comes in a single jet, like water passing through a
narrow hole. In performance, several taps can be turned on at
the same time. Words, silences, sound effects, background music,
facial expressions, gestures, movements across the stage, lighting,
groupings, shadows, shapes and colours in the costume and
décor – all these may be telling us something. At the same time
we are emotionally involved by the appearance, the voice, the
personality of the actors. We may feel in sympathy with one,
hostile to another. The words are all filtered to us through a mesh.

Our awareness of what they mean is inseparable from our awareness of vocal timbre, tone, timing, inflexion and atmosphere. In poetry and fiction, the basic currency is words; in drama it is the physical presence of the actors.

The set and the atmosphere

At a performance of Chekhov's *Three Sisters*, the story-telling starts with the stage picture, and we have picked up quite a lot of information before the first word is spoken. Here are the directions Chekhov gives:

> *The Prozorovs' house. A drawing-room with columns beyond which a ballroom can be seen. Midday. Outside the sun is shining cheerfully. A table in the ballroom is being laid for lunch.*
>
> OLGA, *wearing the regulation dark-blue dress of a high-school teacher, carries on correcting her pupils' exercise books, standing up or walking about the room.* MASHA, *in a black dress, sits with her hat on her lap reading a book.* IRINA, *in a white dress, stands lost in thought.*

If these instructions have been followed, we will first form a composite impression, focusing gradually on the contrasts and details. At the same time as noticing the faces of the three women, we will observe the differences between them in dress, posture and mood. Without noticing that our attention is being divided between them and the background, we will register the overall appearance of the room and the furniture, the midday sunlight outside, the ballroom visible behind the columns, the table being set in the hall. With only a few seconds to absorb all this before we start concentrating on the dialogue, we will form only a vague impression, which can be clarified as the scene proceeds. Our ears stay tuned to the words, while our eyes go on collecting details.

When we read the play, we run the risk of missing most of the atmosphere and the emotional impact that the scene can make. It's like reading a painter's description of his picture instead of looking at the canvas. We may read through the italicized stage direction as if it were a descriptive opening paragraph in a novel, or perhaps even more cursorily, feeling that the play doesn't properly begin until we get to the dialogue. If a novel started with a description, the writer could go on planting subsidiary clauses in his narrative to remind us of the information he had provided. If he used discreet phrases like 'blinking in the brightness' or 'staring unhappily into the dark corner', we wouldn't even feel that he was repeating himself. The playwright feels no need to provide reminders. He is assuming that the set, the lighting, the costumes and the atmosphere that has been engendered will continuously support the words, like the orchestral accompaniment for a song.

What we can do when we are reading a play is make a conscious effort to digest the opening stage direction as if we were an architect considering a client's description of the house he wants us to design for him. He may only catalogue the relevant points: it is for us to form them carefully into a vivid mental picture that will stay with us throughout the ensuing dialogue.

The use of space

Many theatre directors like to have a three-dimensional model of the set in front of them for at least some of the work they do in preparing a production. Without going to the lengths of building himself a model for each play, the reader can habituate himself to thinking of the action in relation to the writer's use of space. A novelist can move his narrative easily from battlefield to boudoir; so can the playwright, but without being able to shrink or expand the stage. He can ask for different areas to be used or lit, he can modulate between different ways of using them, but he does not enjoy the freedom of the novelist and the film director to zoom into an intimate close-up and then out into a wide-angle long-shot.

From the black print on the two-dimensional page the reader of a play imaginatively builds himself a three-dimensional space in which figures are moving about. He may be visualizing actors on a stage or characters in a place. He may be pitching his mental pictures somewhere between the two possibilities, or, without noticing what he is doing, he may be shifting from one intermediate position to another. If he has seen the play in production he will be drawing intermittently on patchy memories. In any case the moving pictures in his mind's eye will sometimes be quite vivid, and sometimes quite dim. Sometimes they will fade altogether, leaving him aware only of words. At the moments when the play is coming to life in his imagination, his inner ear will be involved as actively as his inner eye. The voices and inflexions he hears may belong either to the characters he is imagining or to the imaginary actors who are playing them. Again, he may be shuttling between the two possibilities, and again his imagination will be working better at some moments than others.

One of the advantages of envisaging actors on a stage (rather than characters in a room) is that you are more likely to remember the playwright's basic problem of filling the space at his disposal. A novelist could keep a character alone and motionless for twenty pages, provided that his stream of consciousness was rippling along interestingly. A play may contain many long speeches, but it is not likely to contain many long soliloquies, and whenever there is more than one character on stage, the reader needs to keep them all in mind. The temptation is to concentrate exclusively on whoever is speaking. A character who is listening – or not listening – may be contributing no less to the theatrical effect. In the Council Chamber scene in *Hamlet* (Act One, Scene Two), the Prince is silent but by no means unimportant during the first sixty-four lines of dialogue. He may be wearing black clothes that contrast with the sumptuous colours of the courtiers' costumes. He may be sitting at some distance from the King and Queen. In any case, his silence, his melancholy and his detachment can make as much theatrical impact as any speeches Shakespeare could have written for him.The others are all hanging on the King's words, waiting for opportunities to curry favour by nodding agreement, murmuring approval or laughing obsequiously at a joke. Hamlet's disaffection can make him into the most interesting character on stage.

This is an extreme case, but the good reader can hardly ever afford to forget any of the characters who are on stage. If they are not speaking, what are they doing?

The play as a series of impacts

Like a filmscript or a musical score, the script of a play is intended primarily for the use of professional performers. Unlike the novelist and the poet, the playwright has been counting on other people to mediate between his words and his public. But plays are usually much more enjoyable to read than filmscripts (in which the dialogue tends to matter less) and much more accessible than musical scores, though we do well to think of a text as a score for a series of theatrical impacts, many of which are not verbal. This encourages us to read more slowly, considering each new development in relation to the effect – or complex of effects – it could have on the audience. To receive the full impact of the dialogue, we need to imagine the sound of the spoken words and the edge they could have to cut against the other characters on stage. Often it's helpful to read the play aloud, sharing the dialogue with a friend. Read in this way, *Waiting for Godot* becomes funnier, livelier and much more approachable.

Stage directions about action

Directions governing action need to be treated no less imaginatively than descriptions of sets. Reading the duel sequence in *Hamlet*, for instance, the eye is liable to glide quickly and ungratefully over such directions as '*They play*', '*The Queen falls*' and '*Stabs the King*'. The problem for the reader is partly visual, partly emotional. Apart from Attendant Lords and Ladies, there are six characters on stage: Hamlet, Horatio, the King and Queen, Laertes and Osric. The movement revolves rapidly around the two traps that have been set to catch Hamlet's life: there is poison on one of the swords and poison which the King will put into a cup of wine. With the possible exception of Horatio, all six characters are moving about quite a lot from the moment the duelling starts. Three of them die within twenty-three lines and Hamlet twenty-seven lines later. The reader needs to have an impression of changes in position, in facial expression, in tone of voice. But the hardest element of all for him to imagine is the audience's emotional involvement in the physical action. The stage direction '*They play*' suggests nothing of the excitement that can be aroused by several minutes of grim duelling. Whatever the earlier provocation, Laertes has now put himself into the wrong by making himself a willing tool of the unscrupulous King. A noble prince is fighting against the accomplice of a murderer.

The direction '*Stabs the King*' calls for a much bigger imaginative effort. This is a crux of the tragedy. Hamlet is at last revenging the murder of his father and the seduction of his mother. At the same time he is striking a blow that cuts through all the other knots the plot has tied. Directly or indirectly, the King has caused the deaths of Polonius, Ophelia, Laertes, the Queen and Hamlet himself. Even for the armchair reader the stage direction is satisfying, because it signals that justice is at last being done, but in performance the audience's longing for the villain to be punished has been strengthened by incomparably more powerful tugs of sympathy and hatred. The reader, alone with his book, should never forget how excited Victorian audiences could become, hissing the villain and cheering the valiant hero of a melodrama. *Hamlet* can be still more exciting. In any play the emotions that the writer is aiming to generate are largely dependent on a collective reaction, but the isolated individual can form a lively impression of them if he uses his imagination.

2

Sound effects

The quality of the sound – The build-up – The knocking on the castle
gate – The knocking on the bedroom door

The quality of the sound

A sound effect presents the reader with the same difficulty as a
visual effect: it is very hard to arrive at an accurate idea of its
theatrical impact, or – if a rhythm is involved – of the accumulat-
ing pressure. The word 'knocking' in italic print inside brackets
does not tell us anything about the quality of the sound. How loud
is it? How insistent? How impatient? How is the noise being
made? An iron door-knocker? A mailed fist thumping on a
wooden door?

The build-up

As with stage directions like '*Stabs the King*', the reader who is
trying to imagine the theatrical impact of a sound effect must
always consider it in the context of a developing momentum. Let's
take an example.

The knocking on the castle gate

The knocking on the gate in *Macbeth* is both a minor climax in
itself and part of the build-up towards a major climax – the dis-
covery of the King's murdered body. In any context, loud and
persistent knocking is unsettling for an audience, and in this
murder scene it comes soon after the alarming sound of the bell.
Both interruptions of the nocturnal silence occur when Macbeth
is alone and in a jumpy state. As a soldier, he is used to killing but
not to murder, and his first victim is to be his King.

The bell rings only once, but the sound reverberates ominously through the sleeping castle. Like all good *coups de théâtre*, the effect finds us at once prepared and unprepared. A servant has been ordered to tell Lady Macbeth to strike upon the bell when Macbeth's drink is ready, but since then, twenty-nine lines of blank verse have put us off our guard. Frightened to find that he cannot trust his own senses, Macbeth is clutching at an imaginary dagger, scaring himself (and us) with the nightmarish ideas that are streaming through his brain. The howling of the wolf is the 'watch' – meaning either time-piece or watchman – that alarms 'withered Murder', which moves, like a ghost, 'with Tarquin's ravishing strides'. Macbeth then commands the 'sure and firm-set earth' not to hear his footsteps 'for fear/Thy very stones prate of my whereabout'. So, after starting with the instruction to the servant, the build-up to the sound-effect is developed through these sinister references to unearthly noises. Like any good build-up, it loads the context of expectation with meaningful associations. The clang, when it comes, will give us a jolt which is all the more disturbing if we connect it, half consciously, half unconsciously, not only with the sounds Macbeth has mentioned but with the act of murder.

The triple rhyme bell/hell/knell, which tolls through his next three lines, forges a theatrical link between the raucous noise and the silent act of stabbing.

> I go, and it is done: the bell invites me.
> Hear it not, Duncan, for it is a knell
> That summons thee to heaven, or to hell.

The knocking does not start until the end of the following scene, but the preparation for this climax has already begun. Shakespeare has put our ears on the alert. Lady Macbeth, who has been drinking, is buoyed up with daredevil euphoria, but within two lines of her entrance she has checked herself to listen. There is no sound effect to represent the shrieking of the owl, so she may either have heard it or imagined it, but her metaphor 'the fatal bellman/Which gives the stern'st goodnight' connects the bird with both the bell and the murder. Macbeth shouts 'Who's there? What, ho?' from off-stage. His first question, when he reappears with blood dripping from the daggers, is whether she heard a noise. With his senses over-stimulated, he cannot differentiate between the real voices of the courtiers he overheard praying and the imaginary voice that said 'Macbeth does murder sleep'.

His fear makes her angry and the anger almost restores her earlier confidence, though she may be trying to rally her own spirits with the pun about *guilt* and *gilding* the faces of the grooms with blood to put the blame on them.

Immediately Macbeth is left on his own again, we hear loud knocking at the castle gate. Symbolism? A theatrical image to represent the pricking of his conscience? An exteriorization of his heartbeats? We are more likely to ask ourselves questions of this sort in reading, when (without even being aware that we have stopped) we can look up from the book to think. A performance gives us no means of controlling the rate at which new sensations are forced on us. With the physical impact of the knocking we are already being led towards the next climax, when the door will be opened. Who will come in?

Imagine a theatre full of people unfamiliar with the play. More crucial than any symbolic overtone is the possibility that Macbeth and his wife will be exposed by the newcomer as murderers of their royal benefactor. There they are, with blood on their hands, still wearing yesterday's clothes. He is almost hysterical, she is under the influence of drink. Will they be sufficiently in control to cover their tracks? Why has someone arrived in the middle of the night? Or is it early morning already? Will he be able to guess whodunnit? The spasmodic bursts of persistent knocking heighten the tension.

At first, left alone with the noise, Macbeth is as helpless and confused as he was during his vision of the dagger:

> How is't with me, when every noise appals me?
> What hands are here? ha! they pluck out mine eyes!
> Will all great Neptune's ocean wash this blood
> Clean from my hand? No; this my hand will rather
> The multitudinous seas incarnadine,
> Making the green one red.

He still can't distinguish the real noise from the noises inside his head, or the hand that is knocking from the fantasy hands trying to tear his eyes out. The drops of blood on his hand seem big enough to turn an ocean red. But the knocking reasserts the common-sense world of everyday reality, and when Lady Macbeth comes back, though she still talks in verse, her speech is objective, matter-of-fact. The knocking is 'at the Southern entry' of the castle, and, without having heard his oceanic exaggeration, she optimistically contradicts it. 'A little water clears us of this deed.'

But the man cannot snap so quickly back into the world of day-light facts.

Wake Duncan with thy knocking! I would thou couldst! Anyway, he goes with her to change into a nightgown, so the confrontation with the newcomer is postponed.

We move, instead, into a scene with a comic porter, while the knocking continues. If the noise is as enervating to the audience as it should be, it generates an almost tangible pressure on the Porter from every willpower in the auditorium. Why doesn't he open the door? How long is he going to go on grumbling? Theatrically, the straight line is the unfunniest distance between the two points. Between the intention and the action there is great scope for hesitation and digression. At the same time the noise and the enervation both help Shakespeare to equate the castle with hell:

> Here's a knocking indeed! If a man were porter of hell-gate, he should have old turning the key. (*knocking*) Knock, knock, knock! Who's there, i' th' name of Beelzebub?

Even when the Porter has opened the gate to admit Macduff and Lennox, the clowning goes on.

The action is moving inexorably towards the climax of discovering the dead King's bloody body, but in tragedy, as in a music-hall routine, a climax is more effective if the audience has been made to wait for it. No playwright was ever more expert than Shakespeare in gauging how long to protract a delay, and how much comedy to inject into a tragedy. There are drunken scenes or at least amusing allusions to drunkenness in nearly all the tragedies, and Macduff, who has no reason to suspect a murder, is still in a good enough humour, despite his long wait at the gate, to act as straight man for the Porter's clownish monologue about drink as a provoker of nose-painting, lechery and urine. And so we move on towards the next climax, when once again the bell will clang to sound the alarm that will rouse all the sleepers in the castle.

The knocking on the bedroom door

In Arthur Miller's play *Death of a Salesman*, Willy Loman's son, Biff, has been a schoolboy hero on the baseball field, but unsuccessful in adult life, except as a sexual free-booter. After building up some mystery about the reasons for his failure to settle down, the action has established that the turning point in his life occurred during his boyhood, when he went to see Willy in Boston. After that, he stopped trying, refused to make up the subject he had failed in his exam. Miller has whetted our curiosity about what happened in Boston, but he leaves us in suspense until he has prepared the context for showing why Willy feels responsible for the change that came over Biff. Evidence of the boy's klepto-mania is provided before we flash back to the hotel bedroom, where Willy is with a woman, while the schoolboy Biff is outside, knocking at the door. We are not in suspense, this time, about the outcome, but additional pressure is generated by setting the flashback as an hallucination that occurs while Willy is in the cloakroom of a restaurant where his two sons are entertaining two girls. Miller swings us several times between present and past, introducing the knocking during one of the swings, and then bringing it back like a Wagnerian motif as we settle into the past for the showdown. The woman is laughing at Willy for his reluctance to open the door. He is too frightened even to shout 'Go away'. So the sound effect continues, uncomfortably, for some time before Willy lets Biff in:

WILLY: They're knocking on the wrong door.
THE WOMAN: But I felt the knocking. And he heard us talking in here. Maybe the hotel's on fire!
WILLY (*his terror rising*): It's a mistake.
THE WOMAN: Then tell him to go away!
WILLY: There's nobody there.
THE WOMAN: It's getting on my nerves, Willy. There's some-body standing out there and it's getting on my nerves!
WILLY (*pushing her away from him*): All right, stay in the bathroom here and don't come out. I think there's a law in Massachusetts about it, so don't come out. It may be that new room clerk. He looked very mean. So don't come out. It's a mistake, there's no fire.
(*The knocking is heard again . . .*)

With the woman in the bathroom, Willy could have got rid of Biff before she came out, but characteristically, after telling the boy to go downstairs and wait, Willy procrastinates. In his giggling admiration for Biff's skill in mimicking a schoolteacher, he encourages the boy to repeat the performance. When the woman starts laughing in the bathroom and emerges half-naked, nothing Willy says or does can help. The experience is traumatic for Biff, and Willy has reason to feel guilty. As in *Macbeth*, the physical impact and the psychological resonance of the sound effect are inseparable.

3

Momentum and suspense

The first question we ask of any play is 'Does it come to life?' We don't mean 'Is it lifelike?'; we mean 'Is it alive?' We want it to seem like a growing organism, biologically independent of its creator. We want it to keep moving, but not like a machine that follows a set pattern. We want the movements to be unpredictable and interesting enough to keep our curiosity constantly whetted.

Beginnings

If the narrative flow of a novel is like a single jet of water, the story must start from a single point, and then there can be only one new impact at a time. The reader does not have to concentrate simultaneously on the background and the foreground; there will be one moment for the description of the pattern on the wallpaper, another for the girl's hair, another for what she says. The style of the writing is geared to the linear movements of the reading eye.

The playwright can simultaneously arouse the audience's curiosity in several areas. The silent action at the opening of *Three Sisters* makes us wonder why Olga is so restless. Why doesn't she sit down to correct the exercise books? Why is Masha reading with her hat on her lap? Is she about to get up and go? Will anyone be joining them at the table which is being prepared for lunch?

Unlike the novelist, who is addressing each reader separately – in private, as it were – the playwright must grab immediately at the corporate attention of his audience, implanting the same expectancy all over the auditorium. No hack writer of commercial thrillers has ever shown more skill than Shakespeare in arousing curiosity at the outset, hooking the audience's reactions along the same suspenseful track, scooping hundreds of consciousnesses into the same mood. *Hamlet* begins with a nervous sentry relieving another in front of a haunted castle, and within forty lines a ghost has appeared. *Macbeth* starts with thunder, lightning and witches. At the opening of *Coriolanus* citizens are rioting with clubs and sticks.

A good opening provides an immediate spark of curiosity-whetting vitality, and with most scripts it is apparent quite early on whether the stuff we have in front of us would ignite theatrically. Not that the stage events need to be intrinsically sensational. As the curtain goes up on Oscar Wilde's *The Importance of Being Earnest*, a butler is arranging afternoon tea on a table and Algernon asks him whether he has cut the cucumber sandwiches for Lady Bracknell. At the start of *Death of a Salesman* Willy Loman is coming home, carrying his two sample cases, but something is wrong. His wife wasn't expecting him back so soon. Both beginnings give us something to look forward to: the arrival of Lady Bracknell; the solution of the minor mystery created by Willy's unexpected return.

In the post-war theatre some beginnings have gone to the opposite extreme, as if to make it clear that no surprise packages would be unwrapped in the near future. In Beckett's *Waiting for Godot* the lights go up on two shabby men. One of them is trying to take one of his boots off. Harold Pinter's *The Birthday Party* starts with a woman in her sixties who is shouting through a hatch to tell her deckchair-attendant husband that his cornflakes are ready. At the beginning of Tom Stoppard's *Rosencrantz and Guildenstern are Dead*, two bored attendant lords are whiling away the time by tossing coins.

But at least the playwright has put two characters in front of us. Something must happen. As with two animals in a cage at the zoo, we may not want to watch for very long, but the inclination, nearly always, is to wait until we have seen a sign of the interaction between them. Is anything interesting going to happen?

An argument in the street

Next time you go out of the house, your attention may be caught by an argument in the street. You may even stop to listen, wanting to see how the situation develops. It is potentially dramatic. Even if it is an argument between two people speaking a language you do not understand, the tones of voice, the gestures, the pattern of the interaction may be highly watchable. Possibly the argument will culminate in a fight; possibly they will settle their differences and go off with their arms around each other's shoulders. Or it might peter out, or become boring, as it will if they go on making the same kind of point in the same tone of voice.

Perhaps you are a playwright watching the incident with a view to incorporating something similar into a new play. How will your script differ from your raw material? You are starting with realistic dialogue involving real conflict between real people: what do you have to do to make it dramatic? If you make a cassette recording of the argument on a machine hidden in your raincoat pocket, you will probably hear, when you play it back, moments of dialogue that are excitingly dramatic, even without the angry gestures and indignant expressions you remember having seen. But does the dialogue build theatrically towards a climax? And does that climax lead in the right way to the next?

What is the right way? Or if there are many ways, all equally right, how can we describe them?

The rhythm of progression

One of the main pleasures of poetry is the rhythm, which builds a pattern of expectations that will be partly fulfilled, partly frustrated. The frustrations will themselves be satisfying if the poet strikes an interesting balance between regularity and irregularity. Tennyson's poem *The Lady of Shalott* is boring both in its rhymes and in its rhythms, which hardly ever deviate from regular iambics: di-dum, di-dum, di-dum, di-dum.

> She left the web, she left the loom,
> She made three paces thro' the room,
> She saw the water-lily bloom,
> She saw the helmet and the plume . . .

Browning's poem *The Last Ride Together* is strongly rhythmic but more dramatic – less predictable and closer to the cadences of normal speech:

> Then we began to ride. My soul
> Smoothed itself out, a long-cramped scroll

Freshening and fluttering in the wind.
Past hopes already lay behind.
  What need to strive with a life awry?
Had I said that, had I done this,
So might I gain, so might I miss.
Might she have loved me? just as well
She might have hated, – who can tell?

Rhythms in a play

The rhythms in dramatic dialogue – whether it is in verse or in prose – may be contributing greatly to the audience's pleasure and to the build-up of its expectations, but the very fact that the text is distributed between several speakers complicates the workings of the rhythm, as in this passage from *As You Like It*:

PHEBE: Good shepherd, tell this youth what 'tis to love.
SILVIUS: It is to be all made of sighs and tears,
    And so am I for Phebe.
PHEBE: And I for Ganymede.
ORLANDO: And I for Rosalind.
ROSALIND: And I for no woman.

Other rhythms may be at work simultaneously. To the extent that each actor gives his character an individual tempo of talking, reacting, thinking, moving, each one is different. As the example from *Macbeth* showed us, the bursts of movement towards a climax can themselves constitute a rhythm, while sound effects like knocking or visual effects like a revolving lighthouse beam can introduce another rhythm which is sustained either briefly or through a prolonged sequence.

  The poignancy of the final moments in Chekhov's *The Cherry Orchard* depends on combining different kinds of rhythm. The house has been sold; the cherry orchard is going to be cut down. After the sound effects that represent the family's departure – doors being locked, carriages driving off – there is the first melancholy thud of an axe-edge hitting a tree. Then the sound of dragging footsteps in the house that ought to be empty. The 87-year-old man-servant, Firs, appears in a jacket and white waistcoat, with slippers on his feet. The feeble, faltering rhythm of his final speech suggests that after he lies down he is never going to get up again.

FIRS (*goes up to the door and touches the handle*): Locked. They've gone. (*Sits on the sofa.*) They forgot me. Never mind, I'll sit here a bit. And Mr Leonid hasn't put his fur coat on, I'll be bound, he'll have gone off in his light one. (*Gives a worried sigh.*) I should have seen to it, these young folk have no sense. (*Mutters something which cannot be understood.*) Life's slipped by just as if I'd never lived at all. (*Lies down.*) I'll lie down a bit. You've got no strength left, got nothing left, nothing at all. You're just a – nincompoop. (*Lies motionless.*)

After this we get the final stage direction:

(*A distant sound is heard. It seems to come from the sky and is the sound of a breaking string. It dies away sadly. Silence follows, broken only by the thud of an axe striking a tree far away in the orchard.*)

Because of the distance, the sound is not loud, but the rhythm is merciless.

Argument on a park bench

In contrast to our imaginary argument in a street, let's consider the argument on the park bench in Edward Albee's play *The Zoo Story*. A placid, bespectacled middle-aged man, Peter, was reading his book on the bench until Jerry accosted him, apparently desperate for conversation.

JERRY: Now I'll let you in on what happened at the zoo: but first, I should tell you why I went to the zoo. I went to the zoo to find out more about the way people exist with animals, and the way animals exist with each other, and with people too. It probably wasn't a fair test, what with everyone separated by bars from everyone else, the animals for the most part from each other, and the people from the animals, but, if it's a zoo, that's the way it is. (*He pokes Peter on the arm.*) Move over.

PETER (*Friendly*): I'm sorry, haven't you enough room? (*He shifts a little.*)

JERRY (*Smiling slightly*): Well, all the animals are there, and all the people are there, and it's Sunday and all the children are there. (*He pokes Peter again.*) Move over.

PETER (*Patiently, still friendly*): All right. (*He moves some more, and Jerry has all the room he might need.*)

JERRY: And it's a hot day, so all the stench is there, too, and all
the balloon sellers, and all the ice cream sellers, and all the
seals are barking, and all the birds are screaming. (*Pokes Peter
harder.*) Move over!

PETER (*Beginning to be annoyed*): Look here, you have more
than enough room! (*But he moves more, and is now fairly
cramped at one side of the bench.*)

JERRY: And I am there, and it's feeding time at the lion's house,
and the lion keeper comes into the lion cage, one of the lion
cages, to feed one of the lions. (*Punches Peter on the arm,
hard.*) MOVE OVER!

PETER (*Very annoyed*): I can't move over any more, and stop
hitting me. What's the matter with you?

JERRY: Do you want to hear the story? (*Punches Peter's arm
again.*)

PETER (*Flabbergasted*): I'm not so sure! I certainly don't want
to be punched in the arm.

JERRY (*Punches Peter's arm again*): Like that?

PETER: Stop it! What's the matter with you?

JERRY: I'm crazy, you bastard.

PETER: That isn't funny.

JERRY: Listen to me, Peter. I want this bench. You go sit on
the bench over there, and if you're good I'll tell you the rest
of the story.

The rhythm in the prose is neither regular nor strongly marked,
but the pulse of the dialogue seems to be beating more feverishly
as it moves towards a climax. Certain words are being repeated
again and again – *zoo, animals, people, lion*. The blows on the
arm are becoming harder and the demands more provocative.
There is also a rhythm to the way Jerry keeps swinging between
his description of the zoo and his demands for more space. Is he
an animal caged by his own territorial imperative? Is he really
crazy? The dialogue fans the flames of our curiosity about him.
This is a highly dramatic sequence because the development is
very rapid and we know it cannot go very much further in the
same direction. Either there will be violence or a sudden cooling
of the hostility, a climax or an anti-climax. As with a verse
rhythm, expectations are being aroused which must either be
fulfilled or satisfyingly frustrated. Given sufficient tension, an
audience invariably makes half-conscious forecasts about how it
will be resolved: to be wrong can be just as pleasurable as to be

right. With *The Zoo Story* we are right to predict violence, and it is not altogether surprising when Jerry pulls out a knife, but it is surprising when he tosses it to Peter and when Peter lets himself be provoked into holding it out aggressively. It is more surprising still when Jerry impales himself on it.

Maximum receptivity

How can the reader put himself in a state of maximum receptivity to the multiple rhythms of a play? Theatre directors need to be especially sensitive to the potentialities of a script, but it is almost as hard for them to envisage a production as it is for a conductor to sit down with an orchestral score and imagine the work in performance. I know one theatre director who never settles down to a new script without having a bath, shaving, and putting on a clean shirt, just as if he were going out to the theatre. He takes the telephone off the hook before sitting down in his favourite armchair, and he doesn't get up till he's finished the first act, when he allows himself fifteen minutes before starting on the second.

If a script is a score for a series of impacts, it is important to approximate as closely as you can to receiving them uninterruptedly in the order the playwright arranged them and within the same span of time. A play is hardly ever too long to read at a single sitting, and with any work, new or old, the ideal reader will try to clear his mind of all expectations except those which accumulate as he reads. Each impact will then come as a surprise and each surprise should be considered three-dimensionally. How is it filling the space between the actors and the audience?

Reading like this, you are more alert to the play's rhythms, even if you are not thinking about them in terms of rhythm.

4

Not by words alone

The silence under the words – The conjuror's patter – Visual transformation – The shuffling footsteps – Visual inequalities

The silence under the words

In 1962, making one of his rare speeches, Harold Pinter said:

> There are two silences. One when no word is spoken. The other when perhaps a torrent of language is being employed. This speech is speaking of a language locked beneath it. That is its continual reference. The speech we hear is an indication of that we don't hear. It is a necessary avoidance, a violent, sly, anguished or mocking smokescreen which keeps the other in its place. When true silence falls we are still left with echo but are nearer nakedness. One way of looking at speech is to say it is a constant stratagem to cover nakedness.

Sometimes it is relatively easy for the armchair reader to unlock the language beneath the dialogue. In the final act of *The Cherry Orchard* the family is about to move out of the old house which has been bought by the businessman Lopakhin. There is a sequence between him and Mrs Ranevsky's adopted daughter, Varya, who has been working more or less as a housekeeper. She could look after the house for him if he marries her, as, apparently, he wants to. Alone with Madam Ranevsky, he says:

> If it's not too late I don't mind going ahead even now. Let's get it over and done with. I don't feel I'll ever propose to her without you here.

But this is what happens when he is left alone with Varya:

> VARYA (*spends a long time examining the luggage*): That's funny, I can't find it anywhere.
> LOPAKHIN: What are you looking for?

VARYA: I packed it myself and I still can't remember. (*Pause.*)

LOPAKHIN: Where are you going now, Varya?

VARYA: Me? To the Ragulins'. I've arranged to look after their place, a sort of housekeeper's job.

LOPAKHIN: That's in Yashnevo, isn't it? It must be fifty odd miles from here. (*Pause.*) So life has ended in this house.

VARYA (*examining the luggage*): Oh, where can it be? Or could I have put it in the trunk? Yes, life has gone out of this house. And it will never come back.

LOPAKHIN: Well, I'm just off to Kharkov. By the next train. I have plenty to do there. And I'm leaving Yepikhodov in charge here, I've taken him on.

VARYA: Oh, have you?

LOPAKHIN: This time last year we already had snow, remember? But now it's calm and sunny. It's a bit cold though. Three degrees of frost, I should say.

VARYA: I haven't looked. (*Pause.*) Besides, our thermometer's broken. (*Pause.*)

A voice at the outer door : MR LOPAKHIN!

LOPAKHIN (*as if he had long been expecting this summons*): I'm just coming. (*Goes out quickly.*)

At the beginning of this sequence the girl's embarrassment increases when he fails to speak first. She knows that he knows why she has come into the room, but she still feels compelled to improvise a pretext for being there. The pretence of looking for something among the luggage also gives her an excuse for turning her back on him. Had she been bold enough to look him in the eye and wait for him to speak first, the outcome might have been quite different. He is obviously in two minds about whether he wants her as his wife, and when he inquires about her plans, he may, clumsily and half-heartedly, be leading up to asking her to stay – or he may be uncertain of where he wants to take the conversation. The moment for the crucial question is then allowed to slip by. This cannot accurately be described as either intentional or unintentional. He is not fully in control either of himself or the situation.

Lopakhin's remark about the distance of Yashnevo is just a piece of procrastination, and, after an agonized pause, he is out of his depth and treading water when he says that life in the house has come to an end. His embarrassment exacerbates hers. There is irony in his being able to ask Yepikhodov to stay while he is unable to ask her, but he is reduced to talking about the weather. It is an enormous relief for him when the shout from the yard provides a pretext for leaving the room. There is not a single direct expression of emotion in the sequence, but the audience can gauge what is going on underneath the surface of irrelevant words.

The conjuror's patter

Most conjuring tricks could be performed in silence, but they would be much less theatrical. Without relying entirely on his patter to distract the spectators from what he is doing with his hands, the performer is capitalizing on the fact that their attention is divided. So is the playwright. A good script is incomparably more impressive and interesting than the text of a conjuror's patter, which would be very boring to read, though there may be an ironic contrast between what is being said and what is being done.

In Strindberg's play *The Father*, the mother is trying to drive her husband mad by encouraging his doubts about the paternity of the child, Bertha. He is enraged to the point of threatening that he will kill her, but in the end his old nurse soothes him into letting go of the revolver. She then coaxes his arms into a straitjacket.

NURSE (*enters*): Mr Adolf, what is it?

CAPTAIN (*looks at the revolver*): Have you taken the cartridges?

NURSE: Yes, I've hidden them away. But sit down and calm yourself, and I'll bring them back to you.

> *She takes the* CAPTAIN *by the arm and coaxes him down into the chair, where he remains sitting dully. Then she takes the straitjacket and goes behind his chair,* BERTHA *tiptoes out left.*

NURSE: Do you remember, Mr Adolf, when you were my dear little baby, how I used to tuck you up at night and say your prayers with you? And do you remember how I used to get up in the night to fetch you a drink? Do you remember how I lit the candle and told you pretty stories when you had bad dreams and couldn't sleep? Do you remember?

CAPTAIN: Go on talking, Margaret. It soothes my head so. Go on talking.

NURSE: All right, but you must listen, then. Do you remember how once you took the big carving knife and wanted to make boats, and how I came in and had to get the knife away from you by telling you a story? You were such a silly baby, so we had to tell you stories, because you thought we all wanted to hurt you. Give me that snake, I said, otherwise he'll bite you. And you let go of the knife. (*Takes the gun from the* CAPTAIN'S *hand*.) And then, when you had to get dressed and you didn't want to. Then I had to coax you and say I'd give you a gold coat and dress you like a prince. And I took your little body-garment, which was only of green wool, and held it in front of you and said: 'Put your arms in', and then I said: 'Sit still, now, and be a good boy while I button up the back!' (*She has got the straitjacket on him*.) And then I said: 'Stand up now, and walk nicely, so I can see how you look.' (*She leads him to the sofa*.) And then I said: 'Now it's time to go to bed.'

CAPTAIN: What's that, Nanny? Must I go to bed when I'm dressed? Damnation! What have you done to me? (*Tries to free himself*.) Oh, you damned cunning woman! Who would have believed you were so crafty? (*Lies down on the sofa*.) Caught, cropped, and cozened! And not to be allowed to die!

The scene works on several levels for both the audience in the theatre and the reader. We don't want Bertha to be shot, so there is a thriller-like suspense until the revolver is safely out of the Captain's hand. Underneath this action is a Strindbergian irony which cannot be fully effective for the reader unless he is visualizing the characters in action, using his imagination to create a performance for himself.

The appearance of the old nurse is reassuring: her voice and her presence carry associations of the child's protected existence in the nursery, the room where help is always available and nothing worse can happen than a bump on the head. But the straitjacket in the old woman's hand warns us contrapuntally that her former nursling is in danger. What she says is as soothing as a lullaby; what she does is as unmanning as a castration. Her action reduces the Captain to the defenceless feebleness of the child he was in the nursery. There is double irony – and double bluff – in her reminiscence about having to trick him when he didn't believe they meant well by him. She is tricking him now, but he catches on too late to the contradiction in what she is saying. The speech is calculated to divert attention from what the hands are doing, but the words are also ramming home Strindberg's point that throughout his life the man has been a victim of superior female cunning. The reader can imagine the cosy, comfortable timbre of the old woman's voice, with its coaxing inflexions, while picturing what she is doing to reduce a dangerous-looking male with a revolver into ridiculous-looking helplessness, his arms secured behind his back like a lunatic.

In these sequences from *The Cherry Orchard* and *The Father* there is a wide gap between spoken words and the feeling or purpose underlying them, but in neither passage is it difficult for the actor or for the reader to be sure of how the words ought to be spoken. Like most politicians, the characters are using language not to reveal but to conceal their intentions. We know what Lopakhin, Varya and the Nurse are up to. We also know that all three would talk quite differently if they were really saying what they meant. The irony is visible in the wide space between language and intention, though none of the three characters is conscious of what the playright is saying.

Visual transformation

There can be many different kinds of gap between what is being said and what is being done. In Scene Twelve of Brecht's play *The Life of Galileo*, there is nothing in the dialogue and precious little in the stage directions to tell the reader that a change of costume is producing a change of theatrical identity which effectively amounts to change of personality. Forbidden by the Inquisition to publish his evidence for believing that the earth is not the centre of the universe, Galileo remains silent for eight years. His best friend inside the church has been Cardinal Barberini, a mathematician, sophisticated and tolerant. When he becomes Pope Urban VIII, there seems to be a genuine prospect of ecclesiastical enlightenment. In Scene Twelve we see him giving audience to the Cardinal Inquisitor, who is arguing that the new cosmological ideas constitute a serious threat to the church's authority. The scene opens with three loud shouts of 'No' from the Pope, but while he is being dressed by acolytes in his papal regalia, the Inquisitor does most of the talking. The vestments and papal crown seem to add their weight to the few words that the new Pope utters. After the change of costume is complete, he gives permission for his former friend to be threatened with torture. They may show him the instruments. 'That will suffice, your Holiness,' says the Inquisitor. 'Signor Galileo is an expert on instruments.'

However appreciatively the reader responds to verbal points like this one, he is liable to miss the main theatrical point. The stage direction at the beginning of the scene is casually terse:

An apartment in the Vatican. Pope URBAN VIII, *formerly Cardinal Barberini, has received the* CARDINAL INQUISITOR. *During the audience he is being robed. Outside is the sound of many shuffling feet.*

Before the last two speeches in the scene there is one more stage direction:

Pause. The POPE *is now in his full robes.*

The reader is given no other reminder of what the audience has been watching all through the scene. The Inquisitor will have moved very little, the Pope not at all, but the sumptuous vestments have been reverently handed by acolytes to the senior acolyte, who has reverently been draping them round the body which previously has been much more simply attired. The transformation is a spectacular one, and though Barberini's face does not change, the effect is almost as if he were putting on a mask. The costume is changing him into a Pope. The individual is disappearing into the office. It is Galileo's friend who holds out against the Inquisitor; it is the Pope who submits.

The shuffling footsteps

At the end of the opening stage direction is another sentence which the reader is liable to credit with very much less than its full theatrical value. The shuffling, which goes on throughout the conversation, has an enervating effect on the Pope, which will probably be registered only very casually by the actor. Perhaps an irritated movement of the head; perhaps a hint of tension in the voice. Almost nothing is said about the noise until just before the decision that forms the climax of the scene, when, knowing he is on the point of capitulating to orthodox opinion, the Pope shows his anger, but disguises it, as if the people in the corridor were the only cause. 'This tramping in the corridors is intolerable. Is the whole world coming here?' 'Not the whole world,' answers the Cardinal Inquisitor, 'but its best part.' This is apt because the sound has served to reinforce the first question which the Inquisitor put:

Your Holiness, there are assembled here doctors of all faculties, representatives of all the holy orders and of the whole priesthood who have come, with their childlike faith in the Word of God as revealed in the Scriptures, to receive from your Holiness the confirmation of their faith. Will your Holiness now tell them that the Scriptures can no longer be regarded as true?

These are the strongest sheep in the flock that the shepherd has to consider before answering the question which finally becomes crucial in the discussion. After eight years, Galileo has been allowed to publish his book on condition that the last word is not with science but with faith. The condition has been fulfilled by ending with a dialogue between a stupid man, who believes the sun goes round the earth, and a clever man, who contradicts him. Galileo has contrived to give the last word to the stupid man. In performance, the footsteps unsettle the audience, while they unsettle the Pope with their reminder that the cleverest men in the Church are being unsettled by doubts which Galileo is fomenting.

The writing in this scene is very densely textured. Though the bulk of the argument comes from a viewpoint Brecht dislikes, he lets the Inquisitor make out a very good case. Out of respect for the Pope, he has to choose his phrases carefully, but his logic is intricate and forceful. The reader may need to go through the passage twice – once for the argument and once for the succession of theatrical moments in which the gradual change of costume and the continuous sound effect combine to push the character away from the determination he shows at the beginning of the sequence, exerting considerable vocal energy to say 'No'. As the ceremony of robing proceeds, his stature is visibly enhanced. In other words, his visual dominance in the discussion is being asserted more and more strongly, but he still has to end up saying 'Yes'.

Visual inequalities

Reading a play, our natural tendency is to assume that a character's power depends on his words. If there is nothing to contradict the assumption, we would take it that the one with the most to say is dominant. There is nothing in the text to remind us that in performance, costume, movement and relative positions on stage can enable one character to secure more of the audience's attention than another.

Like the park bench in *The Zoo Story*, the whole stage may be made to seem like a battlefield in which one territorially acquisitive character is competing with another, not for ownership of the space but for ascendancy. Or it may be, as in the duel scene from *Hamlet*, that the action brings first one character, then another, into prominence. The chairs of state on which the King and Queen sit may be on a rostrum and will certainly be in a commanding position. Their costumes confirm their priority in rank, and from the moment of putting Laertes's hand into Hamlet's (Act Five, Scene Two, line 224), the King has established himself as the man who is presiding over the sport. Osric judges the bout and at moments of appeal (e.g. lines 278–9) he is in the centre of focus.

An audience generally tends to focus its attention on whoever is moving or, when there is no movement, on the upstage figure in a group. In a sequence like this one, with a great deal of movement, the focus shifts constantly. Knowing that one of the foils is poisoned, we watch Laertes very carefully when, pretending the one he has taken is too heavy for him, he selects another (line 262). During the duelling, our concentration is likely to be divided equally between him and Hamlet. The first time they break off, it is again the King who claims our attention, when he pops what he says is a pearl into the wine (line 280); the second interruption centres on the Queen, when, after giving Hamlet her napkin to wipe his brow, she drinks from the poisoned cup. The third bout of swordplay brings our attention back to the duellists and momentarily to Osric when he pronounces judgement. The focus then shifts very rapidly from Laertes, who wounds Hamlet when he is off his guard, to Hamlet, who fights furiously for possession of the poisoned foil, and then to the Queen, who falls to the ground.

Hamlet now takes charge of the situation, ordering the doors to be locked. Laertes becomes the centre of attention again when he confesses the truth in an eight-line speech, which culminates in a denunciation of the King. Hamlet then dominates again, stabbing the King and forcing him to drink the poisoned wine. Laertes brings himself back briefly into prominence with his dying speech, but the focus is then on Hamlet until his own death. Horatio is very much the subordinate character, except briefly, when he tries to drink from the poisoned cup.

Domination of a scene does not depend on dominating the other characters: the feeblest of victims may win the lion's share of the audience's attention, and a dying speech is nearly always a big theatrical moment. In the sequence we took from *The Father*, the power shifts from the dangerous-seeming man to the harmless-seeming old woman, but their share of the audience's attention is more or less equal throughout. At the beginning of the sequence from *Galileo*, the Cardinal Inquisitor's costume gives him visual superiority, although Barberini has already been proclaimed Pope. As we saw, the change of costume makes him outshine the Cardinal Inquisitor but, ironically, the more powerful he looks, the less power he has to assert his personal willpower.

5

Costume and identity

*A quick transformation – Dual identities – Disguise – Confusion
without disguise – The prostitute and her cousin*

A quick transformation

The *Galileo* sequence provides a slow-motion sample of a kind of
transformation that is very frequent in drama. Often it involves
disguise. In the last act of Shakespeare's *Measure for Measure*
there is a superb climax when the Duke, who has been disguised
as a Friar, averts a miscarriage of justice. He reveals his identity
by exposing the colourful, opulent, aristocratic costume under the
drab habit which he discards. As with the Cardinal in *Galileo,*
the face remains the same but, theatrically, the identity changes.
A feeble-seeming man, who was about to be led off to prison, is
suddenly the most authoritative figure in the stage picture. The
corruptible Deputy, Angelo, who seemed to have been in sole
control of Vienna, has all the time been under the god-like super-
vision of the disguised Duke.

Lucio has revealed himself as an opportunist who shifts his
loyalties quickly and cynically. He has gossiped with the Friar
about the absent Duke, whom he described as 'a very superficial,
ignorant, unweighing fellow' (Act Three, Scene Two, line 135).
Later, in the presence of Angelo, he denounces the Friar as if he
had been the one to slander the absent ruler.

LUCIO: 'Tis he, my lord . . . Come hither, goodman bald-
pate. Do you know me?
DUKE: I remember you, sir, by the sound of your voice. I met
you at the prison, in the absence of the duke.
LUCIO: Oh, did you so? And do you remember what you said of
the duke?
DUKE: Most notedly, sir.

LUCIO: Do you so, sir? And was the duke a flesh-monger, a fool, and a coward, as you then reported him to be?

Angelo orders the Provost to arrest the Friar, who resists, claiming to love the Duke as well as himself. When Angelo tells Lucio to help the Provost, he plucks at the Friar's hood:

LUCIO: Come sir, come sir, come sir: foh sir, why you bald-pated lying rascal . . . you must be hooded, must you? Show your knave's visage, with a pox to you . . . show your sheep-biting face, and be hanged an hour . . . Will't not off?

The Friar's identity has been no secret from the audience, who could not otherwise have enjoyed the irony in what he says about loving the Duke. Sooner or later the disguise was bound to be discarded, but it is clever to trigger the revelation through the initiatives of the two men who will be discomfited most. As the reader can imagine, the sudden blaze of rich colours from the Duke's costume is like the sun of justice coming out from behind a cloud. The stage picture quickly re-orients itself. Angelo, who had been giving all the orders, is eclipsed; Lucio will be punished for his duplicity and Shakespeare celebrates with a joke:

DUKE: Thou art the first knave that e'er mad'st a duke.

Dual identities

Earlier in the play, when the Duke goes into disguise, Shakespeare is, in effect, loading him with a dual identity. For most of the time that he is dressed like a Friar, he talks and behaves like a Friar. Knowing that he is not a Friar, the audience has the satisfaction of being aware of the distance between the Duke's 'real' character and the role he is playing. It is a case of play-acting inside a play. Similarly, in *King Lear*, Edgar effectively becomes two people – a young nobleman and a half-crazy beggar – while Kent is both an Earl and a servant.

In performance, confusions of identity can be extremely entertaining, and moments of recognition or revelation extremely satisfying, but for the armchair reader, whose contact with the action is not through the physical presence of the actors but through words, it may be hard to understand why so many plays revolve around problems of identity. Why do conventional plots contain so many identical twins, so many babies swapped while still in their cradles, so many men disguised as women and women disguised as men, so many characters who find themselves putting on elaborate performances in response to other people's determination to behave towards them as if they were someone else?

The central character in Gogol's comedy *The Government Inspector* is not a government inspector but a clerk without even enough money to pay his bill at the hotel. Hearing that the landlord is going to complain to the Mayor about him, he threatens to complain about the landlord. A moment later his servant Ossip comes in.

OSSIP: Here – the Mayor's downstairs . . . asking all sorts of questions about you.

KHLESTIAKOV (*terrified*): What? No! That damned landlord's complained already! Suppose he's come to take me to prison. . . ? Well, what of it, they'd have to treat me like a gentleman, and at least there'd be food . . . No! No! I won't go, someone might see me, one of those officers or that pretty little daughter of the seed-merchant I've been flirting with, I can't let them all see me being dragged off to prison. Who the devil does he think he is, anyway, this landlord? I'm not some miserable shopkeeper or smelly labourer! (*Screwing up his courage.*) I'll tell him to his face. 'How dare you!' I'll say. 'Who do you think you are?' I'll say. 'Who the hell are you. . . ?'

The doorhandle turns, and KHLESTIAKOV *grows pale and shrinks into himself. Enter the* MAYOR, *shutting the door on* DOBCHINSKY. KHLESTIAKOV *and the* MAYOR, *both equally terrified, stare at each other in silence for some moments. The* MAYOR *recovers first and comes to attention.*

MAYOR: May I take the liberty of wishing you good-day, sir?

KHLESTIAKOV (*bowing*): Much obleeged, I'm sure.

MAYOR: I hope you'll pardon the intrusion . . .

KHLESTIAKOV: Not at all.

MAYOR: It's my duty, as senior official in the town, to see that all visitors and persons of rank and quality suffer no inconvenience . . .

KHLESTIAKOV (*breaks in, stammering, but raising his voice as he goes on*): B-b-b-but what could I d-d-d-do . . . I'm g-g-going to p-p-pay, I really am, they're sending money from home . . .

Enter DOBCHINSKY, *shutting the door on* BOBCHINSKY.
It's his fault, not mine. The food's uneatable, terrible, the
meat's like shoe leather and the soup, God only knows what
he puts in the soup. I had to throw some out the window just
now. That man's starving me! And the tea . . . you'd never
know it was tea, it stinks like fish-glue! Why should I . . .
why . . . I don't see why . . .

MAYOR (*intimidated*): Please forgive me, it's really not my fault.
The meat in the market's always good, I see to that, it's all
brought in by good honest dealers, we've never had a com-
plaint like this before. I really can't imagine where he could
get bad meat. But sir, if you aren't satisfied with things here,
I'd best escort you to other quarters . . .

KHLESTIAKOV: No, no, no! I know what you mean with your
'other quarters' – you mean the jail. Well, I won't go! You've
got no right, how dare you! I-I-I'm a Government official
from Petersburg, I-I-I

MAYOR (*aside*): Dear God, he's furious! Those damned shop-
keepers have told him everything.

KHLESTIAKOV (*wildly bluffing*): You can bring a whole regi-
ment with you, I still won't go! I'll write straight to the
Minister, I will! (*He thumps the table.*) Who do you think you
are? You . . . You . . . !

MAYOR (*trembling, stands to attention*): Oh, please, sir, have
pity on us, don't ruin us! My wife . . . my little children . . .
it'll ruin us!

Like the other corrupt officials in the town, the Mayor lives in fear
of being found out. Khlestiakov is under no misapprehension
about his identity – only about his motive for coming to the room
– but the Mayor is confused about Khlestiakov's identity. The
comedy has nothing to do with verbal wit, and the reader's enjoy-
ment must depend partly on how vividly he can imagine the
physical details – the appearance of the two men, their changing
expressions, their attempts to look and sound less nervous than
they actually are.

Disguise

It is even harder for the reader to envisage the theatrical effect
when characters are disguising their 'real' personality, not by
putting on a brave face (like Khlestiakov and the Mayor), but
dressing up (like Shakespeare's Duke). It is not only in tragedy

that Shakespeare uses disguise to create dual identity. He makes frequent use of the device in comedy and he is sometimes very perfunctory about the reasons he gives his characters for assuming a false identity: in *Twelfth Night* Viola has no convincing motivation for dressing up as a boy.

The convention that stage disguises are impenetrable is sometimes troublesome to modern audiences. How can King Lear be stupid enough not to notice that his servant Caius is actually the Earl of Kent, who is supposed to be in exile? If Orlando in *As You Like It* really loves Rosalind, how can he possibly fail to recognize her when she is standing next to him, even if she is dressed as a boy? The reader is at an advantage in not having to watch the characters looking at each other, but at a disadvantage in not being able to catch the full flavour of jokes that depend on physical appearance or the full theatricality of recognitions, where the characters may be reacting differently to the revelation.

The Greek dramatist Menander, who wrote in the third century B.C., was the first playwright to make a thorough exploration of how confusion over identity could be exploited. One of Plutarch's anecdotes about him drives home the point that in this kind of play the words are of secondary importance. A few days before a Dionysian festival, one of Menander's friends was concerned that his play was still not finished. 'Yes it is,' said the playwright. 'I've done the plot. Now all I have to do is write the lines.' To the reader, the lines constitute the play: a mere synopsis of the plot is indigestible and extremely boring. But in Menander's plays the words are only trimmings around the structural confusions of identity. The plots contain the germs of countless subsequent farces, comedies, thrillers, films and television dramas. Children have been brought up in ignorance of their parentage; brothers unwittingly flirt with their sisters; husbands make love to their disguised wives in the belief that they are embarking on an exciting adultery; nubile ladies reject eligible bachelors, believing them to be philandering husbands.

Confusion without disguise

The confusion of identity does not need to be based on disguise. Oliver Goldsmith's comedy *She Stoops to Conquer* introduces a rich hero, Young Marlow, who is shy with girls of his own class but feels quite at ease with barmaids. Confronted with the desirable Kate Hardcastle, he is gauche to the point of speechlessness, but a practical joke, played by her boorish half-brother, Tony Lumpkin, convinces Marlow and his friend Hastings that they are in an inn when actually they are in the Hardcastles' house. The confusion involves not only identity but manners. The behaviour appropriate to the paying guest at an inn is not appropriate to the suitor invited to the house of his future father-in-law:

> MARLOW (*After drinking*): And you have an argument in your cup, old gentleman, better than any in Westminster Hall.
> HARDCASTLE: Ay, young gentleman, that, and a little philosophy.
> MARLOW (*Aside*): Well, this is the first time I ever heard of an innkeeper's philosophy.
> HASTINGS: Let's see your list of the larder, then. I ask it as a favour. I always match my appetite to my bill of fare.
> MARLOW (*To* HARDCASTLE, *who looks at them with surprise*): Sir, he's very right, and it's my way, too.
> HARDCASTLE: Sir, you have a right to command here. Here, Roger, bring us the bill of fare for tonight's supper. I believe it's drawn out. Your manner, Mr Hastings, puts me in mind of my uncle, Colonel Wallop. It was a saying of his, that no man was sure of his supper till he had eaten it.
> HASTINGS (*Aside*): All upon the high rope! His uncle a colonel! We shall soon hear of his mother being a justice of peace.

They go on, patronizingly, to tell him what they want for their supper. Later, taking Kate for a maidservant, Marlow tries to flirt with her, succeeding, almost accidentally, in winning her love.

The amorous entanglements in Menander's plots often involve a courtesan or a slave who will subsequently be recognized – probably through a birth-mark – as well-born and therefore marriageable. There have been variations on this theme in plots which give aristocratic heroes different reasons for wooing a girl while in the guise of a low-ranking soldier (as in Sheridan's *The Rivals*) or a humble and penniless student (as in Beaumarchais's *The Barber of Seville*).

Oscar Wilde's sophisticated plotting in *The Importance of Being Earnest* culminates in a characteristically Menandrian revelation: the hero has a noble pedigree, so no one can object to the marriage. At the beginning, when Lady Bracknell interviewed Jack Worthing as a candidate for the hand of her daughter Gwendolen, he could say nothing about his parentage except that he was found in a large black leather handbag with handles, which was erroneously given to Mr Thomas Cardew in the cloakroom of Victoria Station, when he was on his way to the seaside resort that provided the infant with a surname. Lady Bracknell's main function in the play is to represent the social order that rejects foundlings as unacceptable marriage-partners. When it emerges that the handbag contained the infant son of her own sister, she is satisfied.

The other main source of comedy in the play is a different kind of identity-confusion. Jack has been going under the alias of Ernest Worthing when he was in the country, and Gwendolen has declared that she would be unable to love a man with any other Christian name. Cecily Cardew arrives at the same decision after Jack's friend, Algernon Moncrieff (who will turn out to be his younger brother) has introduced himself to her under the same alias, pretending to be Jack's younger brother, Ernest. Cecily and Algernon withdraw into the house together just before Jack arrives in mourning to announce Ernest's death, and when Gwendolen appears, it looks as though both girls are engaged to the same Ernest. Meanwhile both men have arranged with the local clergyman to be christened Ernest, but when Jack comes into the garden, Cecily reveals his identity, and when Algy appears, Gwendolen, his cousin, reveals his. After the dénouement has brought the revelation that Jack is Lady Bracknell's nephew, his name turns out to be Ernest John.

The prostitute and her cousin

Brecht's use of disguise in *The Good Person of Szechwan* could be seen as an anti-Romantic and Marxist inversion of the disguise convention as used in *Twelfth Night* and *As You Like It*. Brecht's prostitute heroine, Shen Teh, appears in a mask and male clothes to sort out the financial troubles that her generosity has caused her. Rewarded by three itinerant gods for the hospitality she has given them, she has been exploited by people who find how easy it is to take advantage of her new affluence. She hasn't the heart to evict the homeless family of eight that comes to camp in her tobacconist's shop, and she is equally at the mercy of the greedy and the needy – landlady, carpenter, tradesmen. To save herself from losing all her money, she resorts to the old comedy stratagem of inventing a relation – a cousin who is a rich and respectable

businessman, Shui Ta. He behaves toughly towards those who
have exploited her inability to say 'No' and he arranges a marriage
for her with a rich barber, Shu Fu.

It is characteristic of Brecht's ironies that later on, when Shen
Teh (wearing her own clothes) strikes up a relationship with
Yang Sun, who wants to be a pilot, his interest in her turns out to
be more financially than romantically motivated. The scene in
which she discovers this – while disguised as Shui Ta – depends
for its effect on the old theatrical device of identity-confusion.
As in the Forest of Arden sequences between Rosalind and
Orlando, the boy fails to realize that he is not only talking *about*
his girl, but *to* her. Shen Teh is willing to sell her shop for three
hundred silver dollars, which Yang Sun needs to bribe his way
into a job as a pilot. He has promised to marry her, but he does not
intend to take her with him to Pekin.

SHUI TA: It costs quite a bit for two.
SUN: Two? I'm leaving the girl here. She'd only be a liability at
    first.
SHUI TA: I see.
SUN: Why do you look at me as if I was something the cat had
    brought in? Beggars can't be choosers.
SHUI TA: And what is my cousin to live on?
SUN: Can't you do something for her?
SHUI TA: I will look into it. (*Pause.*) I should like you to hand
    me back the two hundred silver dollars, Mr Yang Sun, and
    leave them with me until you are in a position to show me two
    tickets to Pekin.
SUN: My dear cousin, I should like you to mind your own
    business.
SHUI TA: Miss Shen Teh ...
SUN: You just leave her to me.
SHUI TA: ... may not wish to proceed with the sale of her
    business when she hears ...
SUN: O yes she will.
SHUI TA: And you are not afraid of what I may have to say
    against it?
SUN: My dear man!
SHUI TA: You seem to forget that she is flesh and blood, and has
    a mind of her own.
SUN (*Amused*): It astounds me what people imagine about their
    female relations and the effect of sensible argument. Haven't

they ever told you about the power of love, the twitching
of the flesh? You want to appeal to her reason? She hasn't
any reason! All she's had is a lifetime of ill-treatment, poor
thing! If I put my hand on her shoulder and say 'You're
coming with me,' she'll hear bells and not recognize her own
mother.

SHUI TA (*Laboriously*): Mr Yang Sun!

SUN: Mr . . . whatever your name is!

SHUI TA: My cousin is indebted to you because . . .

SUN: Let's say because I've got my hand inside her blouse?
Stuff that in your pipe and smoke it! (*He takes another cigar,
then sticks a few in his pocket, and finally puts the box under his
arm.*) You're not to go to her empty-handed: we're getting
married, and that's settled. And she'll bring the three hundred with her or else you will: either her or you. (*Exit.*)

This dialogue relies on the rudimentary dramatic irony of
letting the audience into the secret (which is being kept from
Yang Sun) about the identity of the 'man' he is talking to. As in
Shakespearian disguise scenes, the dialogue loads the emotional
strain on the back of the character in disguise; in *Twelfth Night*
and *As You Like It* we watch the flickering expressions on the
girls' faces as they keep their lovers under the illusion. Watching
a masked character under pressure like this, we sometimes get the
impression that the papier mâché features are moving. Their
rigidity increases the pressure on the audience, which is sympa-
thizing with Shen Teh, knowing how hard she must be fighting
the impulse to rip the mask off. In reality the actress needs to keep
her head fairly still: the mask must move relatively little, but the
audience is projecting its own emotions on the immobile features.
It is not easy for the reader to visualize the effect.

Even when Yang Sun goes, Shen Teh is not alone, so she has
to sustain her impersonation, but she cannot behave consistently.

SHUI TA (*crying out*): The business has gone! He's not in love.
This means ruin. I am lost! (*He begins to rush round like a
captive animal, continually repeating* 'The business has gone!'
until he suddenly stops and addresses MRS SHIN.) Mrs Shin,
you grew up in the gutter and so did I. Are we irresponsible?
No. Do we lack the necessary brutality?

When she reappears in her own person, Shen Teh again allows
herself to be seduced by Yang Sun, in spite of what she knows

about him, in spite of knowing she will get herself into trouble again. The understanding she acquires as Shui Ta is of no use to her when she reverts to being a woman.

In fact the whole conception of Shen Teh depends on the amoeba-like dichotomy that gives birth to Shui Ta. Her goodness consists of freedom from the vices that are necessary to survive in a world corrupted by the profit motive. But she is no less unrealistically simplified than her anti-type, and her theatrical identity when she isn't wearing a mask is created no more realistically than when she is. On the page, her dialogue can seem facile unless the reader is visualizing the contrast between her two personae and imagining what the actress might sound like and look like, mimicking male toughness both vocally and in her movements.

6

Identity and character

The mistake of psycho-analysing – The relationship between the parts – Falstaff – Cause and effect

The mistake of psycho-analysing

It is always a mistake to 'psycho-analyse' characters in plays as if they were real people, and it is a mistake we are likelier to make when we are reading than when we are in the theatre, reacting to physical impacts, liking her face and his voice, amused by one actor's timing, repelled by another's way of twisting his mouth sideways.

The relationship between the parts

All works of art make their main statement through the relation- ship between their component parts, but in a painting all the part· are present to the eye at the same moment. In a novel or a play we have to start at the beginning and work our way to the end, which means there are two basic kinds of relationship. We might call these latitudinal and longitudinal. The *latitudinal* relationships are those which exist simultaneously at any one moment of action, while the relationships involving the passage of time are *longitudinal*. It is, for instance, a longitudinal line that connects the Macbeth we meet at the beginning of the play, the brave and successful warrior, with the desperate villain of the last act.

Questions like 'How many children had Lady Macbeth?' never bother us in the theatre. She says:

> I have given suck, and know
> How tender 'tis to love the babe that milks me –
> I would, while it was smiling in my face,
> Have plucked my nipple from his boneless gums,

And dashed the brains out, had I so sworn as you
Have done to this.

This tells us quite a lot about the latitudinal differences between
her and Macbeth; it does not tell us whether she was different
when she first became a mother or how long ago it was. And the
questions of how many children she had and whether they are still
alive do not matter any more than the question, say, of whether
Macbeth was good at games when he was a boy. They are irrelevant to both longitudinal and latitudinal relationships between the
component parts of the play.

It would be equally senseless to analyse the 'character' of
Brecht's Shen Teh. The play is a 'moral fable', and she is a per-
sonification of goodness. She has plenty of theatrical vitality, and
we sympathize so much with her in her dilemma that we forget
how generalized she is. As a personality she scarcely exists and it is
impossible to imagine her as a character in a novel. It would be
pointless to speculate about her past or about such questions as
whether she derives gratification from dressing up in male clothes.
Her character can't be analysed in terms of repressed aggressions
that find no outlet in her normal sex life. We aren't even required
to take her seriously as a prostitute. It was an amusing idea of
Brecht's to suggest that no one more virtuous could be found,
and to let the gods be embarrassed at the danger of compromising
themselves by giving her money after accepting her hospitality
for the night; but there's no realistic interest in her sexual and
financial dealings with her clients.

Is it because Brecht was writing what he called a moral fable
that the focus is on human behaviour rather than individual
character? Or is the playwright *always* more concerned with
behaviour than with character? Anyway, what does the word
'character' mean? It is a dangerous word because it implies a
coherence, a consistency and an individuality, which may not be
there. When we read a play, the only evidence we have about a
character is the stage directions and the dialogue – what he says
and does and what other people say about him and do to him
during two hours (or so) of stage action. This is quite enough
evidence for constructing an idea of what the play would be like in
performance, but not nearly enough evidence – and not the right
sort – for constructing an idea of an individual human being whose
behaviour can be explained in terms of motivations and psychological patterns.

Falstaff

Sir John Falstaff in Shakespeare's *Henry IV Parts 1 and 2* is one of
the liveliest, funniest, most richly satisfying characters that a
playwright has ever created. But his vitality has nothing to
do with his being 'life-like', and the impression of richness has
nothing to do with the amount of information that Shakespeare
feeds us about him. He is a composite of theatrical conventions
that derive partly from the medieval English morality plays, in
which riotous behaviour would be represented semi-symbolically
by a character called Riot. (Today we would hesitate about apply-
ing the word *character* to Riot, or to Gluttony, Lechery and the
other Deadly Sins who are incarnated in such medieval plays as
Everyman.) Falstaff also stems partly from the tradition of
boastful cowards that goes back to classical comedy, and he is like
a clown whose moralizing turns traditional values upside down.
The improvised charade with Hal in *Part 1*, when Falstaff poses
as the King, prepares us for the reassertion of the moral norm at
the end of *Part 2* – the beginning of a new season.

With the circus clown, as with the character stereotypes in
commedia dell'arte (foolish master, crafty servant, etc.), identity is
suggested *visually*. Falstaff is first of all an old man with a stomach
and a complexion that signal disorderly self-indulgence. Shakespeare is writing ironically when he lets someone so sinful cast so
many stones at Bardolph's red nose. Falstaff says:

> I make as good a use of it as many a man doth of a death's
> head or a *memento mori*. I never see thy face but I think of hell-
> fire, and Dives that lived in purple, for there he is in his robes,
> burning, burning. If thou wert any way given to virtue, I would
> swear by thy face; my oath should be, 'by this fire, that's God's
> angel' . . .

Much of Falstaff's vitality derives from the jokes that Shakespeare puts into his mouth; some from the practical jokes that
Prince Hal and his friends play on him. In the highway robbery
sequence, in *Part 1*, Hal and Poins have no difficulty in exposing
him as a coward when they put on masks to rob him of the money
he has just stolen from the travellers. But Falstaff is never at a loss
for an excuse:

> By the Lord, I knew ye as well as he that made ye. Why, hear
> you, my masters, was it for me to kill the heir-apparent? Should

I turn upon the true prince? Why, thou knowest I am as valiant
as Hercules, but beware instinct – the lion will not touch the
true prince. Instinct is a great matter. I was now a coward upon
instinct.

None of his excuses, his jokes or his attempts at moralizing
have the effect of individualizing him, but in spite of knowing so
little *about* him, we are given the illusion of knowing him extremely
well; he quickly becomes an old friend. (As Hamlet and Cordelia
do. When they die, we should feel something almost like bereave-
ment.) What Falstaff says, what he does and what other people
say about him substantiate our first impression, fleshing out the
cartoon. He is a Humpty Dumpty that all the King's men cannot
pull apart, a balloon that cannot be deflated until we are nearly at
the end of *Part 2*, when his hopes of becoming the royal favourite
are punctured. If Shakespeare had been concerned with the
development of an individual character, this final climax, when
Falstaff is unable to bounce back as he always has before, would
be more important for him than any other. In fact the focus isn't
even on him but on the Prince, who has symbolically put aside
Folly now that the death of his father has made him rise to the
responsibilities of maturity:

> I know thee not, old man. Fall to thy prayers.
> How ill white hairs become a fool and jester!
> I have long dreamed of such a kind of man,
> So surfeit-swelled, so old, and so profane;
> But, being awaked, I do despise my dream.
> Make less thy body hence, and more thy grace,
> Leave gormandizing, know the grave doth gape
> For thee thrice wider than for other men.
> Reply not to me with a fool-born jest,
> Presume not that I am the thing I was,
> For God doth know, so shall the world perceive,
> That I have turned away my former self;
> So will I those that kept me company.
> When thou dost hear I am as I have been,
> Approach me, and thou shalt be as thou wast,
> The tutor and the feeder of my riots:
> Till then, I banish thee, on pain of death . . .

Can we say that Falstaff is merely a symbolic representation of
the riotous inclinations which Hal allows himself as a prince,
only to discipline them when he becomes King? No, Falstaff has

certainly existed in his own right as a dominant character in earlier scenes, and though he is subsidiary during this long speech, the reader should not forget that part of the audience's attention is focused on his reaction to it. He may even have opened his mouth to speak just before the King says 'Reply not . . .' Nor is Falstaff pushed out of the play as summarily as he is dismissed from the King's consciousness. After the royal procession has made its exit, there is a short prose scene with Falstaff, Justice Shallow, Pistol and Bardolph. Even now the deflation is not total:

> Go with me to dinner: come Lieutenant Pistol, come Bardolph–
> I shall be sent for soon at night.

Immediately after this he is arrested, in verse, by the Lord Chief Justice, and Shakespeare's use of verse to end the play confirms the rejection of Falstaff, whose scenes have all been in prose. He belongs irrevocably to a lower mode of consciousness, while Hal has always been capable of moving upwards out of it. This is why he is capable of deciding never again to move downwards into it.

So it would be stupid to adopt a 'psycho-analytical' approach to Falstaff's 'character'. We do not need, for instance, to ask ourselves whether childhood deprivations got him into a routine of compulsive over-eating. His childhood is as irrelevant as Lady Macbeth's children. His plump presence is essential to the story, but any ideas we may form about his offstage development have nothing to do with the play. To say that Shakespeare's characterization of him is 'brilliant' is to say that his identity emerges brilliantly in the context of these two plays. He may appear to exist in sturdy three-dimensionality, but even Shakespeare couldn't resurrect him in a play without Hal. The Falstaff in *The Merry Wives of Windsor* is somebody else of the same shape.

Cause and effect

We could say that Hal develops longitudinally while Falstaff does not. He is no more capable of changing his nature than Riot or Gluttony is. Nor is this merely an example of the survival of medieval stage conventions into Elizabethan drama. Modern plays are equally full of 'types' – the oppressive capitalist, the righteous rebel, the generous whore – characters whose behaviour is effectively determined by the *type* to which they belong.

Longitudinal and latitudinal relationships necessarily inter-
weave very differently in drama from the way they do in a novel.
The novel is committed by its form to looking for causal connec-
tions between actions. We must feel that we are in a better position to understand the behaviour of the characters in Chapter XI
if we remember what happened to them in Chapter I. By the end
of *War and Peace* Natasha has grown into a plump woman very
unlike the girl we met at the beginning, but our sense of knowing
her depends on the information we have been fed about her past.
In Tolstoy's early fiction he usually provided a full physical
description of all the characters on their first appearance, and they
remained more or less the same. But the important characters in
his mature novels are depicted mainly through other people's
reactions to them; and while we progressively come to know them
more intimately, another progression is at work as they develop.

The playwright's form pressures him towards selecting fewer
incidents and against treating character development causally.
When the action of a play is contained within the classical limit of
twenty-four hours, it is impossible for the characters to develop
very much. Even in an epic play that spans twenty years, character development will probably conform to a fairly simple scheme.

With any work of art it may be difficult to distinguish between
the pattern the artist has constructed deliberately and the pattern
we see when we look at it. Our instinct is always to interpret, to
arrive at an understanding of a new perception by fitting it into
the framework of concepts we have used for ordering our previous
experience. 'What is it?' we say, when a child shows us a drawing.
However unrealistic a play is, we always tend to look for patterns,
causal relationships, motivations, which we can interpret by
referring to our knowledge of human behaviour. We are also
liable to make moral judgements. Cordelia is no more of a
'character' than Falstaff, but we are prone to ask ourselves such
questions as 'Couldn't she have been a bit more considerate of the
old man's feelings when he was asking for reassurance about how
much she loved him?'

When we read a play the experience tends to be more intellec-
tual and less emotional than it is in the theatre, and we are more
disposed to *interpret*, more eagerly on the look-out for explicable
relationships between the component parts of the text. With
Cordelia, we would do well to remember that much of the
explanation we are looking for is to be found in the actress's (or
boy actor's) appearance of innocence – a white dress may play an

important part in determining our reaction to her. With Falstaff or
with Shui Ta it may be determined largely by the actor's padded
paunch or the actress's severe-looking male mask.

Even when the playwright wants to weave universal forces into
his text – Nature, the gods, destiny – he will do it through the
characters' experience and the other evidence that can be put in
front of us physically. When the action is confined to personal
relationships, the actor's face and personality may function almost
like a mask, at least in the sense of precluding any question of how
the character became what he is. The plot may demonstrate (as in
Oedipus) that the gods destined the hero to do what he has done
and to become what he is, or (as in Ibsen's *Ghosts*) it may show
that the hero has inherited his physical and mental traits from his
father or mother; but it is still the actor's face, make-up and
physique that persuade us to take it for granted that the character
is the sort of man he looks like. It may then turn out to be the
play's function to disabuse us – to unmask him. The Nurse in
The Father is not what she seems. Shakespeare's interest in Prince
Hal's development may seem to be spread over a longish period,
but there is little realistic detail in it and the moment of conver-
sion, which comes when he rejects Falstaff, is almost as abrupt as
the dropping of a mask or the revelation of a ducal costume under
a drab disguise.

Looking at printed words in a playscript, we're likely to assimi-
late the characterization more in terms of static type than of
developing individuality. Unlike the novelist, the playwright is
envisaging a performance, so he is not trying to put words together in a way that will directly convey an illusion of human
personality. But we may respond by piecing the stage directions
and the lines of dialogue together to construct a tentative portrait
which we can adapt as we collect more evidence. From the
beginning we are probably asking ourselves questions like 'Is
Jerry the sort of man who . . .' 'Is Lady Macbeth the sort of
woman who . . .' Outside the theatre we may be far more resistant
to the notion of human typology, but inside we would find ourselves accepting the convention that links identity to type,
behaviour to appearance. Today it would be as hard as ever to
satisfy an audience with a play in which the sympathetic characters
were ugly and the villains attractive.

7

Irony and ambiguity

Irony in the forum – In the nineteenth-century parlour

Irony in the forum

In the sequences we took from *The Cherry Orchard* and *The Father*, there was a wide gap between words and underlying intentions, though the characters were not being consciously ironical. But when Shakespeare's Mark Antony insists that 'Brutus is an honourable man', he does not want to be believed. Even a reader unfamiliar with *Julius Caesar* would soon realize how the actor could let out the throttle on his scorn through the rhetorical repetitions of the phrase. Brutus, who had the chance to address the crowd first, spoke declamatorily but in prose:

> Romans, countrymen, and lovers! hear me for my cause, and be silent, that you may hear: believe me for mine honour, and have respect to mine honour, that you may believe.

Antony's speech is in verse, which helps the actor to point the deliberateness of the phrasing, while the rhythm makes the repetitions more striking than they could be in prose. The irony in the first reference to 'the noble Brutus' would not be apparent to the unsuspecting reader, but Antony has no sooner used the word 'honourable', than he puts it, effectively, into inverted commas by repeating it in the next line:

> (For Brutus is an honourable man;
> So are they all; all honourable men)

If we are prompted to glance back at the beginning of Brutus's speech, we see that he repeated the word honour as soon as he used it, implicitly suggesting that honour is the crucial issue. After three more 'honourables' and six more mentions of Brutus's name, Antony can easily put his initial praise of the *noble* Brutus into an ironic perspective with a scathing pun about 'brutish beasts'. The first part of Antony's speech ends when he breaks off to weep. He resumes after brief speeches from four of the Plebeians have enabled him to gauge their reactions. The two new allusions to 'honourable men' are blatantly ironic, so the reader, by turning backwards and forwards over about two pages, could see how the hidden intention is determining the actor's tone.

In the nineteenth-century parlour

Some passages of dialogue are much harder to construe without the mediating actor, especially when the playwright is making his characters talk guardedly, with deliberate ambiguity. In Ibsen's *Hedda Gabler*, for instance, during the second conversation between Hedda and Judge Brack, it is obvious that they both mean more than they are saying, but how much more? Even after reading to the end of the play and turning back to re-read the more difficult passages, it is hard to be sure.

At the end of the first act, Tesman, the spectacled, plump, 33-year-old husband has been pleading with his new wife, the 29-year-old Hedda, not to play with the pistols that belonged to her father, General Gabler. As the lights go up on the second act, she is loading one of them and shouting out of the French windows to the 45-year-old judge, who is – perhaps symbolically – using the back way into the house. Teasingly threatening to shoot him, she aims at him and fires, deliberately missing, but deliberately alarming him. This prepares, theatrically, for the verbal duelling that is to follow. Brack says it was stupid of him not to have realized Hedda would be alone in the house. He should have come earlier. Instead of withdrawing, as we might have expected, into cold politeness, she confides in him about the excruciating boredom she endured on her honeymoon while Tesman was researching in libraries and copying out old parchments. She is obviously not in love with him or she wouldn't say:

And there's nothing exactly ridiculous about him. Is there?

For someone so proud, she is surprisingly eager to explain why she accepted his offer of marriage:

BRACK (*looks at her a little uncertainly*): I thought you believed, like everyone else, that he would become a very prominent man.

HEDDA (*looks tired*): Yes, I did. And when he came and begged me on his bended knees to be allowed to love and to cherish me, I didn't see why I shouldn't let him.

BRACK: No, well – if one looks at it like that –

HEDDA: It was more than my other admirers were prepared to do, Judge dear.

BRACK (*laughs*): Well, I can't answer for the others. As far as I myself am concerned, you know I've always had a considerable respect for the institution of marriage. As an institution.

HEDDA (*lightly*): Oh, I've never entertained any hopes of you.

BRACK: All I want is to have a circle of friends whom I can trust, whom I can help with advice or – or by any other means, and into whose houses I may come and go as a – trusted friend.

HEDDA: Of the husband?

BRACK (*bows*): Preferably, to be frank, of the wife. And of the husband too, of course. Yes, you know, this kind of triangle is a delightful arrangement for all parties concerned.

HEDDA: Yes, I often longed for a third person while I was away. Oh, those hours we spent alone in railway compartments –

BRACK: Fortunately your honeymoon is now over.

HEDDA (*shakes her head*): There's a long, long way still to go. I've only reached a stop on the line.

BRACK: Why not jump out and stretch your legs a little, Mrs Hedda?

HEDDA: I'm not the jumping sort.

BRACK: Aren't you?

HEDDA: No. There's always someone around who –

BRACK (*laughs*): Who looks at one's legs?

HEDDA: Yes. Exactly.

BRACK: Well, but surely –

HEDDA (*with a gesture of rejection*): I don't like it. I'd rather stay where I am. Sitting in the compartment. *A deux.*

BRACK: But suppose a third person were to step into the compartment?

HEDDA: That would be different.

BRACK: A trusted friend – someone who understood –

HEDDA: And was lively and amusing –

BRACK: And interested in – more subjects than one –

HEDDA (*sighs audibly*): Yes, that'd be a relief.

BRACK (*hears the front door open and shut*): The triangle is completed.

HEDDA (*half under her breath*): And the train goes on.

Stage directions like '*laughing*', '*lightly*' or '*sighs audibly*' do not help us to understand the hidden language. Does Hedda want Brack to think she might have been interested in an offer of marriage from him? Does he want her to think that he is not interested in her sexually? Is he really not interested in her sexually, or is he interested in friendship mainly as a stepping-stone? What kind of triangular relationship does she have in mind? Is each of them understanding what the other intends and intending what the other understands? Are they calculating seriously how much they want to reveal of their feelings and intentions, or being diverted into an appealingly dangerous game of flirtation? How much are they each staking and how much more would they be prepared to stake?

The dialogue is highly ambiguous, whether you read the play or watch it in performance, but the two sets of ambiguities are quite different. The reader's only evidence is Ibsen's words, but the audience is watching a man and a woman together. Each pause, each hesitation, each inflection, each movement of the head, the hand, the body is providing evidence which is blended with the words before they reach us. We have no time to extricate our interpretation of what is happening from the director's and actors' interpretation of the text. The meaning of a phrase can depend on tone, timing, phrasing, on how she is looking at him, how close he is to her, whether her hand touches his. The actors are interpreting the script in two ways – involuntarily and voluntarily. The involuntary element arises directly out of their personalities – some are naturally more outgoing and seductive than others. What they can control, within the limits of their technique, is the use they make of their voices, eyes, face-muscles, physiques. For each syllable, dozens of tones and movements are available to them, and the choices they make will be based mainly on the work done with the director and the rest of the cast during the rehearsal period. So the audience is looking at the end-product of a long period of interpretative work, whereas the reader new to the play knows nothing about Brack except what he has learnt from the previous act. According to Ibsen's stage direction,

JUDGE BRACK *is forty-five; rather short, but well built and elastic in his movements. He has a roundish face with an aristocratic profile. His hair, cut short, is still almost black, and is carefully barbered. Eyes lively and humorous. Thick eyebrows. His moustache is also thick, and is trimmed square at the ends. He is wearing outdoor clothes which are elegant but a little too youthful for him. He has a monocle in one eye ; now and then he lets it drop.*

Tesman's conversation with his aunt has also revealed that the Judge helped to make arrangements for them to buy the house on easy terms. This action could have been motivated by his interest in Hedda.

The reader's interpretation of the sequence is based on his knowledge of the preceding text; the actors' interpretation is based on the whole play. They know that Hedda is going to kill herself when Brack is in a strategically advantageous position. He finds out that she has given one of her pistols to Eilert Loevborg, who shot himself with it. It is now in the possession of the police, who are trying to trace the owner. Unless Brack keeps silent, Hedda will have to appear in court together with the madam of the brothel where Eilert killed himself. Brack promises not to abuse the power he now has over her, but Tesman will be out every evening, working on the manuscript of Eilert's book with Mrs Elvsted, so Brack will be 'the only cock on the dunghill', as Hedda puts it in her last words before she shoots herself. He hadn't expected her to take this way out of her dilemma and he hadn't deliberately set about creating it for her. It is even possible that he intended to keep his promise about not abusing his power. Ibsen's intention was that each passage of dialogue should be filtered through the actors' personalities and performances. The ambiguities remain, but they are not nearly so wide open as they are for the reader.

Is this openness a disadvantage? Undeniably it makes for difficulties during the first reading, when it is hard to cope with the variety of options the text offers, but for the reader who is willing to take time and trouble, the experience can be fascinating. He even has an advantage over the director in the theatre in that he does not have to find a single practical solution to every problem. The action going on inside his imagination is more like a rehearsal than a performance, in that he can stop it whenever he wants to make his actors experiment with an alternative inflexion or emphasis. He may even recast a role in the middle of a sentence, deciding, for instance, to make Hedda taller, slimmer, more deliberate in her speech and less attractive.

8

Mental theatre

Where to put the stress – Mental scene-changes

The advantages and disadvantages of mental theatre are analogous to the advantages and disadvantages of mental arithmetic: there is a limit to the complexity of the calculations you can make in your head, but there is no limit to the amount of alterations you can make without creating a mess.

Where to put the stress

The example from *Hedda Gabler* showed us that a text may be offering a wide variety of options. Taking a simpler example, let's, for a moment, ignore all the visual factors, considering only the use of voice. In the thirteen-word question

Surely you aren't telling me to go because they might arrive together again?

there is only one word that could not be loaded with the main stress – the word 'to'. The twelve possible stresses are equally legitimate and they produce twelve meanings which aren't entirely different but aren't exactly the same. If you heard the line performed in a play, it wouldn't occur to you that in settling on one reading the actor had rejected eleven others, and even if it did, you wouldn't have time to work out what the others were. There is also the question of how heavy the stress is, and of whether one of the other words is to be spoken with a stress which, though subordinate, gives the word more weight than the other eleven. And we still haven't touched on the various possibilities of tone, tempo and rhythm. The speaker could be sympathetic or sarcastic, concerned or indifferent, amused or exasperated.

If you can be as dependent as this on the director and the actor with thirteen words, how much greater is the part they play in interpreting a whole script?

There is plenty of scope for obscurity and ambiguity in the novel. Critics often disagree violently in their interpretations, but it is much easier for the writer to be explicit about what is going on inside the characters' minds. He can tell us when one understands, misinterprets or fails to grasp what the other is saying or not saying, and he can explain the deductions each makes from the other's behaviour. The playwright may choose to write '*lying*', '*smiling*' or '*hesitating*' as a stage direction, but there is a narrow limit to the amount of information he can convey like this. The medium tends to push him towards making his statements through the dialogue and leaving it to be interpreted differently in each production. This could be called a limitation of the medium, but a great artist can usually turn limitations into advantages. The richness of Shakespeare's, Chekhov's and the best of Ibsen's texts lies partly in ambiguities which only the careful reader can fully explore.

Mental scene-changes

Though it is generally an advantage to envisage a performance on a stage, the imagination is flexible enough to adapt a sequence of the play into a film when the playwright has been limited by his medium in a negative way. Reading Ibsen's *Rosmersholm*, why shouldn't you picture John Rosmer and Rebecca West as they throw themselves into the mill-race? Why restrict yourself to the housekeeper who is looking out of the window and soliloquizing for the benefit of the audience?

> MRS HELSETH: The carriage, miss, is – . (*Looks round the room.*) Not here? Out together at this time of night? Well, well – I must say – ! Hm! (*Goes out into the hall, looks round and comes in again.*) Not sitting on the bench – ah, well! (*Goes to the window and looks out.*) Good heavens! What is that white thing – ! As I am a living soul, they are both out on the footbridge! God forgive the sinful creatures – if they are not in each other's arms! (*Gives a wild scream.*) Ah! – they are over – both of them! Over into the mill-race! Help! Help! (*Her knees tremble, she holds on shakily to the back of a chair and can scarcely get her words out.*) No. No help here. The dead woman has taken them.

This melodramatic speech is a poor substitute for a direct dramatization of the double suicide.

Chekhov had more mastery over his medium than Ibsen, and it is hardly ever a disadvantage in his work that offstage events and objects remain invisible. It is good that we see no more than a glimpse of the cherry orchard through the window; it might be even better if we saw nothing of it. The reality that the scene-painter can give to it is less important than the reality it acquires through the dialogue, which shows clearly how each of the characters remembers it in a different way. Madam Ranevsky feels nostalgic about the pleasure in the blossom-scented sunlight; Lopakhin is aware that a valuable part of the estate has never been commercially exploited. A film of *The Cherry Orchard* which ended with wood-cutters hacking at the beautiful trees would be showing us something which is better left unseen.

What about the descriptions of offstage action in Shakespearian monologues? When you read the final sequence in Act Four Scene Seven of *Hamlet*, do you visualize the Queen as she talks and Laertes and the King as they react? Or do you see the picture that her words evoke?

> There is a willow grows aslant the brook,
> That shows his hoar leaves in the glassy stream,
> There with fantastic garlands did she come
> Of crow-flowers, nettles, daisies, and long purples
> That liberal shepherds give a grosser name,
> But our cold maids do dead men's fingers call them.
> There on the pendent boughs her crownet weeds
> Clamb'ring to hang, an envious sliver broke,
> When down her weedy trophies and herself
> Fell in the weeping brook. Her clothes spread wide,
> And mermaid-like awhile they bore her up,
> Which time she chanted snatches of old lauds,
> As one incapable of her own distress,
> Or like a creature native and indued
> Unto that element. But long it could not be
> Till that her garments, heavy with their drink,
> Pulled the poor wretch from her melodious lay
> To muddy death.

The description is so graphic that even in the theatre, with three well-lit actors in front of us, the stage picture is partly displaced by the picture that the words paint. Without ceasing to see the

Queen, we also see the drowning Ophelia. Without ceasing to listen to the words, we also hear the dying girl's song. When we are reading, the balance between the two pictures and the two sets of sounds may be different, but all four should be present to our imagination. Watching Laurence Olivier's film of *Hamlet*, we may have thought it was a bad lapse of taste to show a horizontal Jean Simmons floating decorously among the tangled leaves and water-weeds, but the imaginary film sequences we interpolate into our armchair reading will accord perfectly with our own taste.

9

Silence

Looking for silence – How to manage without signposts – Silence alongside speech – Silence and the contemporary playwright – Pressures towards silence – The silent killer

As Susan Sontag has pointed out, 'Much of the beauty of Harpo Marx's muteness derives from his being surrounded by manic talkers.' One of the disadvantages of reading a play is that, not being surrounded by manic talkers, we find it tremendously hard to remember how powerful the theatrical effect of silence can be. Unlike silence in the room where we're reading, silence in a performance can exist only as an interruption to the sound. If action is going on, it will derive a special quality from the silence. The sequence may be building towards a climax, and the silence may play an important part in the progression. Even two seconds of hesitation before the word 'Yes' makes it stronger than it would otherwise be, and the effect of the brief silence is inseparable from that of the yes. A prolonged silence can work powerfully if it starts out of a tension and doesn't last long enough to destroy it.

The three basic problems for the reader are
1. to know where the silences come,
2. to gauge their length,
3. to imagine their effect.

Looking for silence

It is easy enough to spot the silences when the writer gives us some such stage direction as '*After a pause*' or '*Hesitating*'. No playwright can ever have been more scrupulous than Harold Pinter in specifying his requirements. Here is a sequence from the first act of *The Caretaker*. Aston, who lives in a house as full as a lumber-room with useless objects, has come home with a shabbily dressed old man, Davies, who indicates that he often sleeps in the open air.

DAVIES: Nothing but wind then.
  (*Pause.*)
ASTON: Yes, when the wind gets up it. . . .
  (*Pause.*)
DAVIES: Yes. . . .
ASTON: Mmmmn. . . .
  (*Pause.*)
DAVIES: Gets very draughty.
ASTON: Ah.
DAVIES: I'm very sensitive to it.
ASTON: Are you?
DAVIES: Always have been.
  (*Pause.*)
  You got more rooms then, have you?
ASTON: Where?
DAVIES: I mean, along the landing here . . . up the landing there.
ASTON: They're out of commission.
DAVIES: Get away.
ASTON: They need a lot of doing to.
  (*Slight pause.*)
DAVIES: What about downstairs?
ASTON: That's closed up. Needs seeing to. . . . The floors. . . .
  (*Pause.*)
DAVIES: I was lucky you come into that caff. I might have been done by that Scotch git. I been left for dead more than once.
  (*Pause.*)
  I noticed that there was someone was living in the house next door.
ASTON: What?
DAVIES (*gesturing*): I noticed. . . .
ASTON: Yes. There's people living all along the road.
DAVIES: Yes, I noticed the curtains pulled down there next door as we come along.
ASTON: They're neighbours.
  (*Pause.*)
DAVIES: This your house then, is it?
  (*Pause.*)

ASTON: I'm in charge.
DAVIES: You the landlord, are you?
    (*He puts a pipe in his mouth and puffs without lighting it.*)
    Yes, I noticed them heavy curtains pulled across next door
    as we come along.

The careless reader may take little notice of these stage directions, thinking 'Oh, that's something for the actor'. It's also something for the reader, who needs as much information as he can get,
not only from the words but from the spaces between them. In this
passage Pinter has used five different indications for the duration
of the pause. Four dots suggests a longer pause than three dots;
'*Pause*' a longer one than '*Slight pause*'. There is also the final stage
direction, which suggests quite a prolonged pause, coming as it
does in the middle of a speech, immediately after a question which
is left unanswered. The reader cannot yet know that uncertainty
about who is the landlord will be a major cause of anxiety to
Davies, but Pinter obviously wants it to be noticeable that Aston
is not answering the old man's question.

The shorter pauses are important for different reasons. They
stress the discontinuity of the conversation, which indicates that
in their different ways the two men are both embarrassed with
each other, and that their preoccupations do not seem to interlock.
The visual puzzle set by their appearance together is not being
explained by the emergence of a plot in which Aston plans to
make use of Davies. On the contrary, the halting, inconsequential
conversation suggests that the play is not going to generate much
suspense of the usual kind. This in itself increases our mystifica-
tion about how we are going to be kept entertained for the next
two hours.

At the same time, the pauses are helping to characterize the two
men, emphasizing not only their shyness but their inarticulateness
and the difficulties each has in following any line of thought, even
if he has begun it himself. Aston does not know how to finish the
sentence which starts 'When the wind gets up it . . .' and he cannot
explain what is wrong with the floors downstairs. Davies does not
want to go on talking about the times he has been left for dead and
the pause before his next sentence heightens the absurdity of it.
That someone is living in the house next door would not be worth
mentioning unless he were desperate for something to say, and
when Aston says 'What?' he is reduced to a gesture and another
unfinished sentence.

How to manage without signposts

Most playwrights are less scrupulous than Pinter in signalling where the silences come and how long they last. Some of the best playwrights, like Shakespeare, give very little information in stage directions. Their dialogue invariably contains all the help we need, but we have to work a little harder to make sure we don't miss it. We must always be on the look-out for questions which (like 'You the landlord, are you?') remain unanswered. Another indication of a pause is a request which is ignored. In Act One Scene Two of *Hamlet*, the King opposes the Prince's declared intention of going back to Wittenberg:

> It is most retrograde to our desire,
> And we beseech you, bend you to remain
> Here in the cheer and comfort of our eye,
> Our chiefest courtier, cousin, and our son.
> QUEEN: Let not your mother lose her prayers, Hamlet,
> I pray thee stay with us, go not to Wittenberg.
> HAMLET: I shall in all my best obey you, madam.
> KING: Why 'tis a loving and a fair reply . . .

In a hasty reading it might not be apparent that there is a pause after 'our son'. The whole court would be waiting with curiosity for Hamlet's reply to the King. The Queen speaks to prevent the silence from becoming too awkward, but the audience must register the awkwardness first. In replying to her, Hamlet still ignores the King, who then decides to ignore the snub. To clarify this it may be necessary to introduce another, briefer, pause after 'madam'. It may cost the King some slight effort to respond so blandly to such rudeness. Or it may not. This is one of the options that Shakespeare leaves open to the actor.

The reader should also be on the alert for speeches that begin in the middle of a blank verse line. In his mature plays Shakespeare never breaks the line without a good reason, and sometimes the reason is the need for a pause. In the final scene of *Measure for Measure*, soon after the Duke has thrown off his disguise, he condemns Angelo to death for abusing his authority. He has threatened Isabella that unless she sleeps with him, her brother, Claudio, will be executed for inchastity. When Mariana, Angelo's wife, pleads for her husband's life, Isabella does not yet know that Claudio is still alive:

MARIANA: O, Isabel . . . will you not lend a knee?
DUKE: He dies for Claudio's death.
ISABELLA: Most bounteous sir,
    Look, if it pleases you, on this man condemned
    As if my brother lived.

Peter Brook achieved tremendous suspense in his 1951 production of the play at Stratford-on-Avon by making Isabella hesitate in an agony of indecision before kneeling down to plead for the man who has wronged her.

Another sign of the need for a pause is a change of tone. In an earlier scene (Act Three Scene One) in *Measure for Measure*, Isabella tells Claudio about Angelo's threat. She does not intend to submit:

ISABELLA: Be ready, Claudio, for your death tomorrow.
CLAUDIO: Yes. Has he affections in him,
    That thus can make him bite the law by th' nose,
    When he would force it? Sure it is no sin –
    Or of the deadly seven it is the least.

There are two changes of subject (and of tone) in Claudio's short speech. The 'Yes' is an apparently resigned response to Isabella's admonition. The question shifts to speculation about the human emotions of the man who can manipulate the law in his sexual blackmail. The last sentence is a general speculation about fornication: Claudio is thinking both of the offence he has committed in sleeping with Juliet and of the way Angelo would be jeopardizing his own salvation if Isabella submitted to him. The three sections of the speech should be separated by pauses.

The fact that Claudio's first blank verse line is incomplete suggests that there should also be a pause before the 'Yes'. It is not easy to say yes to a command like this one.

Silence alongside speech

There is another kind of silence which is easily forgotten – the silence that exists (like Harpo Marx's) alongside speech. There is nearly always more than one character on stage, and if they all talked at the same time we'd understand nothing. One way of judging an actor's quality is to watch how he listens. A very small movement or a change of rhythm or the inhibition of a movement already in progress can be more telling than a demonstrative reaction.

A good playwright, like Chekhov, works continually through
the complex of pressures that the actors will exert on each other,
not just through words but underneath and around them. A
movement across the stage or a refusal to look someone else in the
eye or to respond to a provocation can say as much as a line of
dialogue.

The main climax in Act Three of *The Cherry Orchard* is the
revelation that Lopakhin has bought the estate, but it is difficult for
the reader to gauge the theatrical impact of the news because
Chekhov, as so often, is making more capital out of what his
characters do not say than of what they do. Without lapsing into
silence, they tread delicately around the edge of it, talking about
irrelevant trivialities or complaining that they feel tired.

It is characteristic of Madam Ranevsky that she should be
holding a party on the evening her estate is up for sale, and the
two-edged mood is established for the whole of the third act as the
curtain goes up on the orchestra which is playing in the vestibule
while couples come dancing downstage into the drawing-room.
Varya, partnered by the Station Master, is weeping quietly,
wiping away her tears as she dances. Gayev, Madam Ranevsky's
brother, should have arrived back from town: unless the auction
has not taken place, the estate must have been sold by now, but it
is just possible that he has bought it himself with the power of
attorney and the money their great-aunt sent from Yaroslavl.
Later on, Anya, Madam Ranevsky's daughter, comes in with news
from the kitchen. An old man said the orchard had been sold but
went away without saying who bought it.

Like Shakespeare, Chekhov often works comedy into the most
dramatic moments, and Lopakhin is greeted on his entrance with
an accidental blow from the stick Varya has been brandishing at
Yepikhodov, the accident-prone clerk. Lopakhin and Gayev have
travelled back together from the auction, but Gayev has not yet
appeared, and instead of coming out with the news that everyone
is waiting for, Lopakhin grumbles about the bump on his head,
about a feeling of dizziness, which may be due partly to brandy,
and about missing the train on the return journey. As in the scene
with the Porter in *Macbeth*, the comedy of procrastination is preparing for a climax which may be tragic. When Gayev enters,
wiping away tears, he seems equally disinclined to talk about the
auction, though Ranevsky, who is also in tears, implores him to
tell her quickly. He makes a gesture of resignation and, still weeping, hands over parcels of shopping. The anchovies and the Black

Sea herrings remind him how hungry he is. Still without answering the question, he goes off to his own quarters, ordering Firs, the old man-servant, to help him change his clothes. It is only after all this that the climax is detonated, when Ranevsky puts two direct questions to Lopakhin:

MRS RANEVSKY: Was the cherry orchard sold?
LOPAKHIN: It was.
MRS RANEVSKY: Who bought it?
LOPAKHIN: I did.

All the previous talk has been necessary to the characters as a smokescreen and to the writer as a build-up, elaborate but not over-extended.

Gayev and Lopakhin had different reasons for not wanting to talk about the auction. Gayev was grief-stricken and guilty about his ineffectuality in preventing the loss of the family's estate, while Lopakhin, according to the stage direction, was *'embarrassed, fearing to betray his delight'*. His silence was also the culmination of the confusion he registered in the play's opening moments. After staying up to meet the family at the station, he fell asleep in an armchair. He has been well disposed towards Madam Ranevsky ever since he was a boy of 15, when she was kind to him after his father had clouted his ear, and throughout the first two acts he has importuned her with well-meant advice about making the orchard into plots for summer bungalows. Now he is the beneficiary of the inertia from which he failed to budge her. An extraordinary theatrical effect is gained out of the two men's reluctance to talk. A playwright less sensitive to ambivalence – and less adept at exteriorizing it – might have given Lopakhin a gloating entrance that would have pricked the bubble too quickly. Victorian melodramas which rush simplistically from one climax to the next are easier to read but much less interesting.

With *The Cherry Orchard* the reader should resist the inclination to concentrate least on the characters who say least and he should keep trying to visualize the changing focus of the stage picture. As soon as Lopakhin comes in, he is the centre of attention. Wherever he sits or stands, this must become the dominant position because the other characters, hanging on his words, will gravitate towards him and group themselves around him. By the time Gayev enters, it is clear that Lopakhin doesn't want to talk, so their curiosity now fastens itself on to Gayev, who remains

dominant only briefly because he remains on stage only briefly.
His exit shifts the centre of gravity back to Lopakhin, who is once
again the only character on stage in possession of the information
they all want. Just as the onstage characters are focusing first on
Lopakhin, then on Gayev, then on Lopakhin again, irrespective
of who else is speaking, so are the spectators in the auditorium. In
Measure for Measure, when the Duke was revealed under the
Friar's habit, there was one abrupt shift in the focus of the stage
picture; here there are three. It is not easy for the reader to make
sufficient allowance for this.

Even in a play like *Hedda Gabler*, where Ibsen grants his
heroine a pre-eminence Chekhov does not allow to any of his
characters in *The Cherry Orchard*, it is all too easy for the reader
to concentrate on what is being said by other characters, forgetting
to visualize Hedda's silent reactions. The more subtly a play's
ironies are developed, the less necessary it becomes for points to
be made explicitly, and when Judge Brack brings the news of
Eilert Loevborg's suicide, there is no need for Hedda to say very
much. The inept and uncomprehending reactions of the others
work almost like spotlights, forcing us to concentrate on her
expression:

HEDDA: Eilert Loevborg has settled his account with life. He's
had the courage to do what – what he had to do.
MRS ELVSTED: No, that's not why it happened. He did it
because he was mad.
TESMAN: He did it because he was desperate.
HEDDA: You're wrong! I know!
MRS ELVSTED: He must have been mad. The same as when he
tore up the manuscript.
BRACK (*starts*): Manuscript? Did he tear it up?
MRS ELVSTED: Yes. Last night.
TESMAN (*whispers*): Oh, Hedda, we shall never be able to
escape from this.
BRACK: Hm. Strange.
TESMAN (*wanders round the room*): To think of Eilert dying like
that. And not leaving behind him the thing that would have
made his name endure.
MRS ELVSTED: If only it could be pieced together again!
TESMAN: Yes, yes, yes! If only it could! I'd give anything –
MRS ELVSTED: Perhaps it can, Mr Tesman.
TESMAN: What do you mean?

MRS ELVSTED (*searches in the pocket of her dress*): Look. I kept the notes he dictated it from.

HEDDA (*takes a step nearer*): Ah!

TESMAN: You kept them, Mrs Elvsted! What?

MRS ELVSTED: Yes, here they are. I brought them with me when I left home. They've been in my pocket ever since.

TESMAN: Let me have a look.

MRS ELVSTED (*hands him a wad of small sheets of paper*): They're in a terrible muddle. All mixed up.

TESMAN: I say, just fancy if we could sort them out! Perhaps if we work on them together – ?

MRS ELVSTED: Oh, yes! Let's try, anyway!

TESMAN: We'll manage it. We must! I shall dedicate my life to this.

HEDDA: *You*, George? Your life?

TESMAN: Yes – well, all the time I can spare. My book'll have to wait. Hedda, you do understand? What? I owe it to Eilert's memory.

HEDDA: Perhaps.

TESMAN: Well, my dear Mrs Elvsted, you and I'll have to pool our brains. No use crying over spilt milk, what? We must try to approach this matter calmly.

MRS ELVSTED: Yes, yes, Mr Tesman. I'll do my best.

TESMAN: Well, come over here and let's start looking at these notes right away. Where shall we sit? Here? No, the other room. You'll excuse us, won't you, Judge? Come along with me, Mrs Elvsted.

Tesman knows already that it was Hedda who destroyed the manuscript, but he does not know the reason. She made out that it was for his sake, so that his reputation should not be eclipsed. Neither he nor she is going to disabuse the others, who still think Eilert tore the book up himself. Hedda cannot give any of them a hint of how much Eilert meant to her, though one of the forces pushing her towards suicide is the irony of her husband's sheepish decision to devote his life to the memory of his former rival. He is partly motivated by eagerness to expiate her guilt in destroying a masterpiece out of loving concern for his reputation.

Hedda is condemned to silence, even when she realizes that the innocuous-looking Thea Elvsted, deprived of her man, is being presented with the same stepping-stones in a relationship with Tesman. The progress from amanuensis to inspiration to mistress may be quite an easy one, especially with Hedda out of the way. The better the actress who plays Hedda, the more subtly her changing expressions register the ironies, which are too complex for a reader to take in without turning to the end of the play and then turning back to this passage – not to study the words but the spaces in between them. Hedda's 'Ah' is a sign of nervousness on Ibsen's part, as if even the actress might need a reminder that she mustn't stop acting just because she isn't talking. Her silent reaction is more important than the words she's reacting to; nor should we forget Brack's reactions when he is not speaking.

Silence and the contemporary playwright

It could be said that twentieth century writers have delved further than their predecessors into the theatrical possibilities of silence. Beckett and Pinter are probably the two most important of the playwrights whose technique has been influenced in its development by experience of radio drama, where silence simply negates a character. In Pinter's first radio play, *A Slight Ache*, there is one character whose very existence is uncertain. After hearing a husband and wife talking to each other about a match-seller, we hear each of them talking to him and becoming increasingly irrational as he fails to answer. They offer him more and more of what they own and give away more and more about themselves, but we never find out whether he has any 'real' existence outside their imagination. His silence, in any case, is acting as a powerful catalyst on the action.

Pressures towards silence

Pinter's first full-length play, *The Birthday Party*, moves ineluctably towards a climax in which the central character is reduced to a theatrical impotence which is expressed by a silence quite unlike that of the powerful match-seller. Meg, the landlady in the squalid seaside boarding-house, chats incessantly, but unlike her husband, Petey, who responds monosyllabically, Stanley begins by talking back to her. It is the two sinister visitors to the boarding-house, Goldberg and McCann, who reduce him to silence. We see them trying to intimidate him in several sequences during Act Two, but we never learn what happens off-stage.

The hardest sequence for the reader to picture is crucial to the third act, which builds up slowly towards Stanley's entrance. We get our first indication that something unusual is happening when Petey discourages Meg from going up to call him. When she went up earlier, she was intercepted by McCann, Goldberg's Irish henchman. Now they are both in the room with him. Next we learn that a big car is waiting outside. Alone with Goldberg, Petey asks how Stanley is. Goldberg talks cheerfully but evasively about his 'nervous breakdown'. The suggestion that Goldberg and McCann may have induced it is strengthened by McCann's qualms. He tells Goldberg he's not prepared to go back into Stanley's room, and there are sinister overtones in the mention of Goldberg's friend Monty as the doctor best suited to treat Stanley. Goldberg seems anxious to get rid of Petey before Stanley comes downstairs; Petey seems too concerned about Stanley to hurry off to work. A comic diversion is provided by Goldberg's scene with Lulu, the girl he seduced the night before, but most of the act is building steadily towards Stanley's entrance:

MCCANN *goes to the door, left, and goes out. He ushers in* STANLEY, *who is dressed in striped trousers, black jacket, and white collar. He carries a bowler hat in one hand and his broken glasses in the other. He is clean-shaven.* MCCANN *follows and closes the door.* GOLDBERG *meets* STANLEY, *seats him in a chair, right, and puts his hat on the table.*

A cursory reading of the stage direction may not be enough to form an impression of the impact made by the change in Stanley's appearance. Previously he has always looked slovenly, unshaven and not very clean. We first saw him coming down to breakfast in spectacles and a pyjama jacket. But in becoming clean and neat, he seems to have lost the knack of taking any initiative. He is the main focus of audience attention as Goldberg and McCann talk to him, simulating concern, while he remains impassive. Goldberg's initial questions are like pebbles dropped into water which makes no plopping sound.

How are you, Stan?
Pause.
Are you feeling any better?
Pause.
What's the matter with your glasses?
GOLDBERG *bends to look.*
They're broken. A pity.
STANLEY *stares blankly at the floor.*

In the long ensuing sequence he remains silent, not even moving or reacting as they bombard him with banter – no doubt from positions on either side of him which would normally be theatrically subordinate.

GOLDBERG: From now on, we'll be the hub of your wheel.
MCCANN: We'll renew your season ticket.
GOLDBERG: We'll take tuppence off your morning tea.
MCCANN: We'll give you a discount on all inflammable goods.
GOLDBERG: We'll watch over you.
MCCANN: Advise you.

They go on in this vein for so long that it's quite hard, even in the theatre, to be sure of whether they're trying to break Stanley down still further or are merely playing with him, like two cats with a mouse they've crippled. The sequence culminates in direct questions which force Stanley into a desperate effort to speak. First his head lifts very slowly to turn towards Goldberg. Then, according to the stage direction,

STANLEY *begins to clench and unclench his eyes.*

In the subsequent stage directions,

STANLEY's *hands clutching his glasses begin to tremble . . .*
STANLEY *concentrates, his mouth opens, he attempts to speak, fails and emits sounds from his throat . . . They watch him. He draws a long breath which shudders down his body. He concentrates . . . His head lowers, his chin draws into his chest, he crouches . . .*
STANLEY's *body shudders, relaxes, his head drops, he becomes still again, stooped.*

I have not quoted the intervening dialogue, which consists of words imitating the inarticulate sounds Stanley makes and of ironically encouraging questions from Goldberg and McCann. Clearly, at this juncture, the words are less important than the action which shows that the central character can no longer use words meaningfully.

The silent killer

Silence has never been a more effective theatrical catalyst than at the end of Eugène Ionesco's *The Killer*, which is like *A Slight Ache* in making a man go on talking into a silence while becoming increasingly unbalanced by his failure to elicit a response from another man, who may exist only inside the imagination.

Like *Macbeth*, *The Killer* illustrates the desolating instability of the relationship between the world inside the mind and the world outside. In both there are powerfully destructive forces, which are seen in the long final soliloquy to be coming together. Ionesco leaves the director free to decide whether the hero, Bérenger, should be talking to himself, alone in the half light, or whether the Killer should appear. If so, '*he is very small and puny, ill-shaven, with a torn hat on his head and a shabby old gaberdine; he has only one eye, which shines with a steely glitter, and a set expression on his still face; his toes are peeping out of the holes in his old shoes*'. He shrugs his shoulders and chuckles softly, but never utters any other sound during Bérenger's speech, which takes up eleven of the script's hundred pages.

Bérenger is walking along a road between the country and the town, where the mysterious Killer has evaded the authorities' half-hearted attempts to hunt him down. The previous action has (intermittently) built up a thriller-like suspense which the audience would expect – expectations being based on previous experiences in the theatre – to reach its climax in an exciting sequence that will show the Killer being cornered. Perhaps he will be arrested or killed; perhaps be will claim another victim – Bérenger. Ionesco is more concerned to show how the enemy inside joins forces with the enemy outside. Whether the Killer is present or absent, chuckling or silent, Bérenger is talking mainly to the elements in his own disposition that refuse to accept the liberal humanist values that his conscious mind affirms.

The monologue starts confidently. With all the arguments of common sense on his side, Bérenger seems stronger than his adversary in every way. What right does the Killer have to cut off other people's chances of happiness? Does he think happiness is impossible? Is he a pessimist, a nihilist, an anarchist? Does he hate women? Think the human race is rotten? Or kill out of kindness to spare his victims from the suffering that life has in store for them? Or to cure their fear of death? Or does he hate mankind, believe the existence of the universe to be a mistake?

Getting no reaction, Bérenger threatens that he has law and order on his side. He is beginning to lose his self-control, while his silent adversary seems quite unaffected by his insistence that Christ died on the cross for him, out of love:

If Christ's not enough for you, I give you my solemn word I'll
have an army of saviours climbing new Calvaries just for you,
and have them crucified for love of you! . . . They must exist
and I'll find them! Will that do?

(*Chuckle from the* KILLER.)

Do you want the whole world to destroy itself to give you a
moment of happiness, to make you smile just once? That's
possible too! I'm ready myself to embrace you, to be one of your
comforters; I'll dress your wounds, because you *are* wounded,
aren't you? You've suffered, haven't you? You're still suffering? I'll take pity on you, you know that now. Would you like
me to wash your feet? Then perhaps you'd like some new
shoes? You loathe sloppy sentimentality. Yes, I can see it's no
good trying to touch your feelings. You don't want to be
trapped by tenderness! You're afraid it'll make a fool of you.
You've a temperament that's diametrically opposed to mine.
All men are brothers, of course, they're like each other, but
they're not always alike. And they've one thing in common.
There must be one thing in common, a common language . . .
What is it? What is it?

Bérenger has already talked himself into an untenable position.
Having baited his hook with the promise that mutual understanding must be possible, he will end by sinking the hook into his own
flesh. He concedes that the Killer has the right to deny love and
think charity a cheat. But what is the purpose of the killing he does?
What use can he make of the fear it wins for him? Bérenger
tries to tempt him with offers of money, friendship, introductions
to girls. By now he is finding the silence almost intolerable.
Like Pinter's characters in *A Slight Ache*, he is helpless to stop it
from acting on him like a negative spur, pushing him backwards
into confession.

Often, I have my doubts about everything too. But don't tell
anyone. I doubt the point of living . . . the meaning of life, doubt
my own values and every kind of rational argument. I no longer
know what to hang on to, perhaps there's no more truth or
charity. But if that's the case, be philosophical; if all is vanity,
if charity is vanity, crime's just vanity too . . . When you know
everything's dust and ashes, you'd be a fool if you set any store
by crime, for that would be setting store by life . . . That would
mean you were taking things seriously . . . and then you'd be in
complete contradiction with yourself.

Can a mouth that says nothing contradict itself? The contradiction is in the words that Bérenger has fed into the silence. If he goes on talking long enough, he cannot avoid contradicting himself. Not yet realizing that he's trapped himself, he tries to laugh at the Killer, ridiculing the idealistic belief in crime which forces him to take all the trouble of killing people without any prospect of deriving benefit from it. The laughter dies on Bérenger's lips, trumped either by the continuing silence or the unvarying chuckle. Soon he is kneeling in front of the Killer, admitting his ignorance.

> It's possible that the survival of the human species is of no importance, so what does it matter if it disappears . . . perhaps the whole universe is no good and you're right to want to blast it all, or at least nibble at it, creature by creature, piece by piece . . . or perhaps that's wrong. I don't know any more, I just don't know.

Even then, though, while there may be no reason to stop killing, he could still stop without having a reason, and this is what Bérenger pleads for. Won't he desist just for a month, a week, forty-eight hours? The Killer's response is to pull out his knife. Bérenger's immediate reaction is to become extremely aggressive. (If the Killer is invisible, the change is abrupt enough to show that he has given up all hope of conciliation.) He produces two pistols from his pocket, aiming at the Killer. But his anger, fuelled only by a chuckle, or by silence, has to run out soon. He can't shoot. There's nothing he can do, except wait for the end.

This sequence creates a tremendously powerful theatrical image, though its only components are an actor (or two) and an empty stage. The speech is not so much a monologue as a conversation with the Nothingness, which is given an almost perceptible existence by the space that surrounds Bérenger. If the actor is (as Hugo von Hofmannsthal once said) 'the mask of God, the one who suffers for the others', the Killer is the mask of the void, the one who inflicts the suffering inherent in the human condition. The director's decision about whether he should be physically present or not is only a decision about whether the mask should be visible or invisible.

As with the Ghost in *Hamlet*, Banquo's ghost in *Macbeth* and the ghosts that appear to Brutus in *Julius Caesar*, the reader's problem is very different from that of the director, who can't have things both ways, as the reader can, letting his imagination shuttle between the alternatives. But, like so many sequences that take full advantage of the medium, Bérenger's speech is far from easy to read. In a generalized way the reader can guess at its theatrical potential as a duet with an unresponsive and possibly non-existent partner. But it is no easier for him to conjure an impression of an empty space from his visual imagination than an impression of silence from his auditory imagination. Bérenger is on stage for a very long time, going through a wide emotional gamut from extreme confidence to extreme desperation, from triumph at cornering the man who killed the girl he loved to suicidal surrender. What would the theatrical effect be like from moment to moment? How much of a mocking echo would the silence give back?

Meaning and experience

What the writer wrote – What does it mean? – A pre-natal examination – The meaning and the experience – From the root experience to the collective reaction – The writer's intentions – What about ideas? – The general and the particular – The generalized salesman – Waiting for the end – The murder of liberal humanism?

What the writer wrote

One of the greatest advantages a reader has over audiences is that he's closer to the writer's original work. Not necessarily closer to his original conception, which may have been more in the form of images or emotional tangles than words, but there, printed on the page, are the words the playwright chose in the order he arranged them. The rhythms that rise up from the page are his rhythms, unaffected by the director's ideas, the actors' personalities, the designer's way of dividing up the space. If we get the impression that Hamlet is hesitating, picking his way through a maze of contrary impulses, this is an illusion thrown up not by an actor's timing but by Shakespeare's words and rhythms. These can be squeezed by a bad production into a wrong-headed interpretation; with a new play, unless we can read it for ourselves, we may find it hard to make up our minds whether production and acting are doing justice to what the writer wrote.

What does it mean?

There is one inescapable difficulty. If we ask ourselves the question 'What does it mean?' when we are sitting in an auditorium, we do not expect the same kind of answer as we do when sitting in an armchair with a book in our hands, at liberty to stop and think whenever we like, or to re-read a difficult passage. Consider Lucky's speech in Beckett's *Waiting for Godot*:

Given the existence as uttered forth in the public works of
Puncher and Wattmann of a personal God quaquaquaqua with
white beard quaquaquaqua outside time without extension
Who from the heights of divine apathia divine athambia divine
aphasia loves us dearly with some exceptions for reasons
unknown but time will tell and suffers like the divine Miranda
with those who for reasons unknown but time will tell are
plunged in torment plunged in fire whose fire and flames if that
continues and who can doubt it will fire the firmament that is to
say blast hell to heaven so blue still and calm so calm with a
calm which even though intermittent is better than nothing . . .

What this communicates in performance is very different from
what it communicates in print. The audience rapidly abandons all
hope of understanding or even construing what Lucky is trying to
say. He has already been on stage for about twenty-five minutes
mutely and slavishly obeying the orders of a bullying master, who
keeps him attached to a rope. After such a protracted silence, we're
taken very much by surprise when he begins to speak. Nor are we
allowed to concentrate on what he is saying. Here are Beckett's
instructions for the behaviour of the onstage audience:

(1) VLADIMIR *and* ESTRAGON *all attention,* POZZO *dejected
disgusted.* (2) VLADIMIR *and* ESTRAGON *begin to protest,*
POZZO's *sufferings increase.* (3) VLADIMIR *and* ESTRAGON
attentive again. POZZO *more 'and more agitated and groaning.*
(4) VLADIMIR *and* ESTRAGON *protest violently.* POZZO *jumps
up, pulls on the rope. General outcry.* LUCKY *pulls on the rope,
staggers, shouts his text. All throw themselves on* LUCKY *who
struggles and shouts his text.*

Lucky would, in any case, probably be speaking too fast for the
audience to form more than a vague idea of what he is saying, and
certainly there is no worry – as there is for the armchair reader –
about where the punctuation would come if there were any, about
who Puncher and Wattmann are, about what *athambia* means,
about whether the Miranda is Miranda in *The Tempest* (who
suffered with those she saw suffer) and about the relative positions
of the fire, the flames and the firmament. We can tell ourselves that
we aren't meant to be in a position to answer these questions, but
if they intrigue us, why should we stop ourselves from struggling
with them?

Admittedly, they are unusually puzzling, but there are many speeches in the work of playwrights as diverse as Shakespeare, Strindberg and Stoppard which are not easy to digest immediately, whether we are hearing them or reading them. My point is that in the theatre we have no option but to content ourselves with the initial impact. Our intellect is not allowed to work separately from our emotions and our senses. In the quiet of our homes we may have to make a decision about how long we are to spend on solving the mysteries and whether to go out to the nearest reference library for information about Puncher and Wattmann.

A pre-natal examination

With a poem or a novel we can argue that it means what it means, irrespective of what its author intended it to mean. We must judge the achievement, which has an objective existence in print. If the work of art is alive, it is alive in its own right.

To read a play is more like conducting a pre-natal examination. Every production is a new birth, even if the mother has been dead for centuries. Some mothers are more explicit than others about how they want their children to be staged, but, as Peter Brook has written in his book *The Empty Space*,

> A word does not start as a word – it is an end product which begins as an impulse, stimulated by attitude and behaviour which dictate the need for expression. This process occurs inside the dramatist; it is repeated inside the actor. Both may only be conscious of the words, but both for the author and then for the actor the word is a small visible portion of a gigantic unseen formation. Some writers attempt to nail down their meaning and intentions in stage directions and explanations, yet we cannot help being struck by the fact that the best dramatists explain themselves the least. They recognise that further indications will most probably be useless. They recognise that the only way to find the true path to the speaking of a word is through a process that parallels the original creative one. This can neither be by-passed nor simplified.

In modern theatrical practice it usually is simplified because the rehearsal period isn't long enough for director and actors to do all the necessary work, even if they are capable of it. Not only are there countless ways of speaking any sentence, there are as many of joining it up with what preceded it: the actor should make his choice after working his way to an understanding of the pressures underneath it. Only then can he judge whether the words are intended to reveal, to edit, to camouflage or to conceal what is going on inside the character.

But what about the reader? Does he have, ideally, to proceed along a path parallel to the original creative one? If it is true that he cannot properly understand the text without envisaging the impact of a performance, it follows that he needs to know how the words should be spoken. Does that mean he must be able to find his way to the mixture of memories, desires, ideas, beliefs and intentions that were in the dramatist's mind at the time of writing? Am I saying we should settle down to read Michael Meyer's biography of Ibsen before starting on *Hedda Gabler*? Certainly not. The best evidence of what was in Shakespeare's mind at the time of writing *Hamlet* is the text itself. This is not to say that Shakespeare's opinions about the human condition were identical with his hero's, but that an internal process has surfaced in the words, the silences, the rhythms and the actions of the play. All we need to know about it can be learned from study of its component parts and the relationships between them.

The meaning and the experience

In *The Dry Salvages* T. S. Eliot wrote:

> We had the experience but missed the meaning,
> And approach to the meaning restores the experience
> In a different form . . .

As we saw when looking at Lucky's speech, the danger for the armchair reader of a play is to have the meaning but miss the experience. Approach to the experience restores the meaning. A play begins in personal experience and its main intention is to convey experience – not necessarily the same, but necessarily not unrelated – to an audience. The reader is like the actor in that he cannot fully enter into what the text is offering unless he can relate it to his own experience. He may be drawing on his previous experience as a reader, on memories of family life and love affairs and on stories other people have told him about their experience, but the play will make sense to him only if he can take it over from the writer, appropriate it, savour it by empathizing.

Consider the directness of children's participation in the theatrical experience. When they want to scream out to Red Riding Hood that a wolf is lying in wait for her in her grandmother's bed, it is not because they have ever found a wolf in their own Grannie's bed but because the story links up with other fantasies that have frightened them. At a performance of *Hamlet* there may be no danger of our shouting out a warning that Laertes is fighting with a poisoned rapier, but if we are emotionally involved in the experience, our anxiety is not altogether unlike that of children at a pantomime. Certainly we are feeling something that the armchair reader cannot feel. The ideas of fratricide, incest and murderously foul play in a duel are not going to work him into a fever of hatred and indignation while he sits quietly looking at superb blank verse in black print on white paper. What he can do and should do is remind himself frequently that Shakespeare was writing for a collective reaction.

From the root experience to the collective reaction

Much of the material a playwright uses derives directly from personal experience, but the private meaning it has for him exists simultaneously in his brain with the public meaning he wants it to acquire in performance. Consider what happens when Hedda Gabler burns Eilert Loevborg's book. Loevborg is a talented, passionate man whom she has rejected, opting to spend her life with the boring Tesman. As a child, Hedda had envied the beautiful hair of another schoolgirl, Thea. Although Thea has since become Loevborg's intimate friend, Hedda, who does not want to become a mother, is less jealous of their physical intimacy than of its productivity. By burning the book she can punish Thea for the part she played in bringing it into existence:

> I'm burning your child, Thea! You with your beautiful, wavy hair! (*She throws a few more pages into the stove.*) The child Eilert Loevborg gave you. (*Throws the rest of the manuscript in.*) I'm burning it! I'm burning your child!

Ibsen's wife, Suzannah, who was fifty-three when he wrote the play, had once been admired for her beautiful hair, and like Hedda, who has decided to reject passion in favour of sedate domesticity, Ibsen had recently decided to stay with his wife instead of travelling round the world with the passionate young girl who was offering herself to him. When he wrote the speech I have just quoted, he was probably thinking simultaneously of the girl, his wife's hair as it used to be and as it was now, of his own decision to stay with her, of his life as it might have been if he had taken the opposite decision and of the theatrical effect that would be created by the sequence he was writing. He may also have been thinking about why he had only one son. According to one witness, Suzannah had said she would not bear him any more children. So the complex meaning that the text had for him was quite different from the meaning he wanted it to convey in performance.

The writer's intentions

This is one reason for being very careful when we talk about a playwright's intentions. Though the audience would be unable to analyse the ingredients of the book-burning scene Ibsen would probably not have written it as he did if he had not wanted to come to terms with painful private experiences. He may have been feeling guilty about staying unadventurously with his wife, or he may have been partly unconscious of his own reasons for bringing all these themes into his play. Discussions of a playwright's 'intentions' usually disregard the fact that the process of writing is largely compulsive.

The involuntary elements in it are not in evidence, so the voluntary ones tend to be exaggerated by biographers, critics and examination papers. The writer may be more or less in control of the technical and more superficial elements, but he is no more in control of the process by which he creates a play than he is of his personality, or his past life. Heathcote Williams described the experience of writing his play *AC/DC* by saying 'I just happened to be a radio set on a certain circuit'. Or, as Pinter put it in a speech at the National Student Drama Festival in 1962, 'You arrange *and* you listen, following clues you leave for yourself, through the characters. And sometimes a balance is found, where image can freely engender image and where at the same time you are able to keep your sights on the place where the characters are silent and in hiding. It is in the silence that they are most evident to me.'*

*See also page 120 of Ronald Hayman: *Harold Pinter*, Heinemann (UK) 1975 (third edition) & Frederick Ungar (US) 1973.

What about ideas?

In 1895 Bernard Shaw opened his campaign for the 'New' Ibsenite theatre, 'theatre as a factory of thought, a prompter of conscience and an elucidator of social conduct'. In March 1950 Terence Rattigan took this statement as his starting point for an attack on 'The Play of Ideas' which he launched in the *New Statesman*, and the controversy lasted till May. James Bridie, Peter Ustinov, Benn Levy, Sean O'Casey and finally Shaw himself contributed articles on 'The Play of Ideas'. Each playwright whipped up his own mixture of sense and nonsense; Shaw's, of course, was the most persuasive and the most dangerous. Plays must be all talk, he said, so how could the talk have no ideas behind it? A fair debating point, but it does not follow that 'The quality of a play is the quality of its ideas'. The ideas in Jean-Paul Sartre's plays are far superior to the ideas in either Arthur Miller's or Ionesco's, but their plays are better than his. It isn't the ideas in Shakespeare's plays that have excited audiences, readers and scholars all over the world for nearly four centuries. It is the way they are expressed.

But we should be careful to differentiate between the ideas – philosophical, political, social, religious – that are tucked explicitly into the dialogue of a play and its overall idea, which may not be at all explicit. *Idea* is not even the best word; *meaning* is better but still not ideal. The didactic purpose of a play by Brecht or Edward Bond is not necessarily identical with what it communicates. Theatrical ideas, images and rhythms have their own way of talking to an audience, which does not always accord with the writer's conscious intention. A condemnation of war and violence may serve partly as a pretext for handling material which is intrinsically more attractive to the writer than he realizes. His treatment of it may, despite his intentions, reveal an ambivalence which he cannot control. Here the reader has more freedom than the director, who may be obliged (if the writer is alive) to produce a compromise between the play the writer intended to write and the play he actually wrote. The reader can concentrate entirely on the one he wrote. (If there is a preface, don't read it until afterwards.)

The general and the particular

To interest the public, a play's relevance must extend some

distance beyond the private experience of its author, but it is difficult to measure how far *Death of a Salesman* is about selling in general, or how far *Waiting for Godot* is about the human condition, or how far *The Killer* is about the impotence of liberal humanism. But these questions must not be ignored.

The generalized salesman

Arthur Miller's play has a lot to say about salesmen in general. Willy's surname is a portmanteau of *low* and *man*, and he is unmistakably a representative of the thousands who earn a living out of sales-talk, without ever quite earning enough to pay off the mortgage on the house they raise their family in. The Willy in the script is sufficiently individualized to make us care about him personally. We can see that he was stupid to commit himself so deeply to the phoney values of salesmanship, losing the capacity to discriminate between a line of patter and a serious promise, but we feel sorry for him as we do for a caged leopard. An animal that in different circumstances could be formidable is looking pathetic, and his cubs are growing up in the same imprisoning confusion.

Reading the play we are more aware of the neatly carpentered slots that interrelate so many images of claustrophobia; in performance we are merely exposed to their emotional pressure. The set should make the home look fragile, encircled with solid apartment blocks, dwarfed by angular towers. The play's opening puzzle about Willy's unexpected return is solved when he complains of being incapable of driving beyond Yonkers. He feels boxed in and his mind is playing tricks. He thinks the windows are all shut when they aren't and that he's been driving with the windshield open when it doesn't open on his new car. All these elements in the first act prepare for the knocking sequence, set claustrophobically in a flashback inside a gents' cloakroom, and for Willy's crazy attempt to plant seeds by torchlight in his yard.

Reading the play we are more likely to become aware of the schematic structure by which the brother and the neighbour are set up to incarnate alternative modes of life. In performance they are merely men who seem less likeable than Willy, so it is quite understandable when he rejects the opportunities they offer him. Ben, the tough, confident, authoritative brother, who made a fortune in Alaska, has given Willy a chance to escape from the airless city to a pioneering life which could have made him happier and richer. Charley, the kind-hearted, law-abiding, wisecracking neighbour later offers him a job when he is out of work, but he is too proud to accept, though not too proud to go on borrowing money from him. Charley, always sceptical about the popularity that the Loman boys' athletic prowess wins for them, brings his son up very differently. In the flashbacks Bernard is a bookworm; in the present tense he has thrown off this unattractive mask to become a successful lawyer and father, while Biff and Happy are still floundering unhappily in the affairs that follow on from impressing girls with a line of talk that is very much like sales-talk. The play's social criticism may be more punchy in per-formance, but it is clearer in reading. Even the recurrence of the word 'dream' in the stage directions works as a reminder that Willy's fantasies are not purely private. The nightmare from which he escapes into suicide is the American Dream.

One advantage of writing social criticism in dialogue form is that you can advance contradictory arguments without needing to make your balance-sheet balance. During Miller's restaurant sequence, the waiter comes out with a neat variation on the Marxist point that commerce is a form of theft. A family business is best, he says. ''cause what's the difference? Somebody steals? It's in the family. Know what I mean?' Miller is at an even further remove than his character from explicitly endorsing the Marxist viewpoint, and while a playwright can use this technique defen-sively to introduce ideas unpalatable to his audience, he can also use it creatively to explore his own ambivalences. The 'How do I know what I think till I see what I write?' attitude is still more viable if you are writing dialogue.

Waiting for the end

Waiting for Godot is one of the plays that tend to make people come out of the theatre with a strong desire to read the text they have just heard in performance. They have probably felt mysti-fied, intrigued, stimulated by the strange resonance of the stylish dialogue and the curious vagueness of the characters, who are as absent-minded about what happened yesterday as they are un-certain about where they are today.

Is it in some sense a religious play? It cannot be accidental that the name Godot is so close to God. Admittedly the play was

written in French, and admittedly Godot had already been used as
a surname by Balzac; but Beckett, who was brought up in
Dublin, would be unable to write 'Godot' without thinking
separately of the first syllable. There are also explicit references to
the two thieves and the crucifixion, to salvation, to the existence of
a personal God with a white beard, to the possibility of comparing
oneself with Christ, to the fire and flames of hell, to blessedness,
and to Cain and Abel. When the boy says that he thinks Mr
Godot's beard is white, Vladimir's response is 'Christ have mercy
on us!' After the boy has gone, Estragon asks what would happen
if they dropped Godot, and Vladimir answers 'He'd punish us'.
In an interview with Harold Hobson,* Beckett said that he 'soon
lost faith. I don't think I ever had it after leaving Trinity.' But the
doctrines and parables that permeated his mind as a child went on
to permeate his work. He also told Harold Hobson: 'One of
Estragon's feet is blessed, and the other is damned. The boot
won't go on the foot that is damned; and it will go on the foot that
is not. It is like the two thieves on the cross.'

Though *Waiting for Godot* is by no means a 'play of ideas' in
Terence Rattigan's sense, it is constructed around ideas which
could be explicated intellectually. In fact they had all been for-
mulated discursively in Beckett's short study of Proust (1931).†
That art is the apotheosis of solitude. That there is no com-
munication. That speech is always either falsified by the speaker or
distorted by the listener. That our memories of the past are no
closer to what actually happened than images produced by our
imagination. That neither we nor our ambitions are the same as
they were yesterday. That there can be no achievement because
the subject can never be identified with the object of his desire.
That time doesn't pass but stays around us like a continuum.

The central idea of the play is its ambiguous image of the
human condition. The act of waiting is itself a contradictory
combination of doing nothing and doing something. We are all
trapped between birth and death, condemned to consciousness;
Vladimir and Estragon seem to be trapped on stage. Where are
they? A country road with a single tree looks more desolate than if
there were no trees at all. Is the tree standing in for Nature?
Is it the whole earth? There's nothing to force them to stay, but
there's nowhere for them to go. The only way out is death, the

*International Theatre Annual No 1, Calder 1956.
†I've analysed the books relationship to the play in *Samuel Beckett*,
Heinemann (UK) 1967, Frederick Ungar (US) 1974.

only relief is night. If they're incapable of suicide or of any other action and if Godot goes on failing to appear, waiting for him is equivalent to waiting for nightfall, for death, or just for the end of the play.

In *Hamlet*, as in *A Midsummer Night's Dream*, the presence of a play within the play works like a mirror focused in on the theatrical situation. In *Waiting for Godot* the implicit acknowledgement of the audience's presence works in the same way. Are we any less trapped than the actors or the characters? There we are, sitting there, and unless we opt out of it by leaving, we have to wait. Doing nothing or doing something? Waiting for Godot or waiting for the final curtain? This is an aspect that the armchair reader can easily forget. And for the audience in the theatre, part of the suspense hinges on the difficulty of guessing how the playwright will manage without the ordinary machinery of suspense. How will he make nothing go on happening for two hours?

Is it a play about nothingness? The single tree and the empty stage play a larger part in the audience's experience than the reader is likely to allow for. The audience will be aware of them all the time; the reader will be reminded of the tree only when Vladimir and Estragon wonder whether they're waiting by the right one, where they arranged to meet Godot; when they try to hang themselves from it; and when they inspect it in Act Two.

The murder of liberal humanism?

The emptiness of the stage at the end of *The Killer* works in very much the same way. If the director decides to give Bérenger an invisible opponent, the sequence works like a contest between an argument and an empty space: Christianity and liberal humanism versus the void.

Bérenger's speech is full of traditional ideas, and superficially it might seem that Ionesco is trying to refute them by showing them to be ineffective. But his concern is theatrical, not philosophical. Bérenger is not the most persuasive of spokesmen for the viewpoint he champions, and his argument is designed to be full of flaws. It is hard for the reader to guess whether the scene would be funny or frightening or both at the same time or sometimes one and sometimes the other. Much depends on the actor, but a very interesting blend can be achieved.

Play-reading as a pleasure

Hazel-coloured hair – To sum up

Hazel-coloured hair

The interest of the public in reading scripts is a new pheno-
menon. Bernard Shaw had been writing plays for eighteen years
before he found a publisher for them. 'The English people had for
a whole century absolutely refused to read plays,' he wrote in a
letter to his German translator, Siegfried Trebitsch, in 1903. 'I
then set to work to make plays readable.' Instead of listing the
characters at the beginning of the published script, he introduced
each one on his first entrance with a description 'as elaborate . . .
as those of Tolstoy and Turgenev'. He boycotted all the technical terms of the theatre, not even allowing himself an 'Enter' or
an 'Exit', and he provided lengthy, leisurely stage directions con-
taining the most detailed specifications. Describing John Tanner
in *Man and Superman*, he wrote:

> a certain high chested carriage of the shoulders, a lofty pose of
> the head, and the Olympian majesty with which a mane, or
> rather a huge whisp, of hazel coloured hair is thrown back from
> an imposing brow, suggest Jupiter rather than Apollo. He is
> prodigiously fluent of speech, restless, excitable (mark the
> snorting nostril and the restless blue eyes, just the thirty-
> secondth of an inch too wide open), possibly a little mad.

This is not written for the director, who is not going to worry
about Greek gods or hazel-coloured hair when he casts the part,
or for the actor, who is not going to calculate how wide his eyes are
open when he plays it, but for the reader, who needs both to be
entertained and to be encouraged to visualize with a maximum of
precision.

In the letter to Trebitsch, Shaw claimed that 'one of the

most important things I have done in England is to effect a reform in the printing of plays'. He certainly did more than any other playwright towards reinstating the drama with the reading public, and the habit of play-reading has since become even more widespread than it was when he died in 1950. Successful playwrights today can easily find a publisher, and the most successful plays may go on selling at the rate of fifteen to twenty-five thousand copies a year.

When John Arden's play *Serjeant Musgrave's Dance* was produced at the Royal Court in 1959, it played to almost empty houses. Though it has since been staged by Peter Brook in Paris, revived at the Royal Court and by repertory companies, it cannot have been seen in performance by more than a few thousand people, while perhaps a hundred thousand copies of the printed edition have been sold, many to libraries, which probably means that the play has been read by at least a hundred times as many people as have seen it on the stage.

But the contemporary playwright has not copied Shaw's practice of attempting to communicate directly with his readers. Stage directions are still printed with almost telegraphic economy, and the fact that readers are not deterred proves that they are quite willing to use their imagination.

To sum up

Everything I have said in this book could be summed up in the sentence 'Imagine a performance as vividly as you can.' In the cultural situation we are now in, television is one of many pressures which tend to make us use our imagination less. It is easier to tune in to a serial than to read a play. But when we do – as when we listen to a play on the radio – we find that there is great pleasure to be derived from allowing our imagination to do the work of contributing all the visual elements.

Please skip the remainder of this chapter if you don't like repetition, nor do I want my résumé of such practical advice as there is in the ten previous chapters to sound like ten commandments. But for those who would like to have a summary of it, here it is:

1. Try to remind yourself of what the set might look like, what sort of atmosphere it would evoke, how the action would fill the space, how the impacts – separately or simultaneously – would affect the audience. Read all stage directions especially carefully.

2. With sound effects, try to imagine the quality of the sound and the way it might help the development towards a climax.

3. Try to make your mind as receptive as possible to the growth of the play's rhythms and the relationships between them.

4. Don't take the words at their face value. Their main function may be to make it possible to reach through them to what lies underneath.

5. Try to think less in terms of character than of identity and of the way it is presented physically.

6. Never psycho-analyse the motivations of the characters as if they were real people.

7. Take time to explore the ambiguities of a script and don't try to close questions the playwright wants to remain open. You *can* have it both ways.

8. Explore and exploit all the opportunities of mental theatre. The best actors and the best equipped theatres in the world all have their limitations. Your imagination can do everything you allow it to. Be generous with it.

9. Look out for the silences, whether they're signposted by stage directions or not. Unanswered questions, ignored requests, broken blank verse lines and changes of tone are no less significant than '*Pause*' or '*Silence*'.

10. A play does not always mean what the writer means it to mean. The meaning is the resultant force that emerges from the words, the silences and all the other elements, and from all the relationships that develop between them.

Key to extracts

For the plays the date in brackets is that of the original performance. The other date is that of the publication.

41 Nikolai Gogol, *The Government Inspector* (1836), Tr.
    Edward O. Marsh and Jeremy Brooks, Methuen, 1968,
    pp. 43–4.

44 Oliver Goldsmith, *She Stoops to Conquer* (1773), in *Four
    English Comedies*, Penguin, 1950, pp. 256–7.

46 Brecht, *The Good Person of Szechwan* (1943), Tr. John
    Willett, Eyre Methuen, 1965, pp. 52–4.

49 Shakespeare, *Macbeth*, I, vii, 55–9.

51 Shakespeare, *King Henry IV Part 1* (*c.* 1598), III, iii, 29–35.

51 ibid., II, iv, 264–70.

52 Shakespeare, *King Henry IV Part 2*, V, v, 48–64.

53 ibid., 89–91.

56 Shakespeare, *Julius Caesar* (*c.* 1600), III, ii, 13–16 and 83–4.

57 Henrik Ibsen, *Hedda Gabler* (1891), Tr. Michael Meyer,
    Eyre Methuen, 1974, pp. 58–60.

59 ibid., p. 49.

62 Ibsen, *Rosmersholm* (1887), Tr. R. Farquharson Sharp,
    The Pretenders, Pillars of Society and *Rosmersholm*
    Everyman, 1913, pp. 315–16.

63 Shakespeare, *Hamlet*, IV, vii, 165–182.

66 Pinter, *The Caretaker* (1960), Methuen, 1960, pp. 11–12.

68 Shakespeare, *Hamlet*, I, ii, 115–21.

69 Shakespeare, *Measure for Measure*, V, i, 437–41.

69 ibid., III, i, 105–110.

71 Chekhov, *The Cherry Orchard*, p. 99.

72 Ibsen, *Hedda Gabler*, pp. 108–9.

75 Pinter, *The Birthday Party* (1958), *The Birthday Party and
    Other Plays*, Methuen, 1960, pp. 85–6 and 87.

78 Eugène Ionesco, *The Killer* (1959), *Plays, Vol. III*, John
    Calder, 1960, p. 104.

82 Samuel Beckett, *Waiting for Godot* (1953), Faber, 1956, p.
    42.

83 Peter Brook, *The Empty Space*, MacGibbon and Kee, 1968,
    pp. 12–13.

84 T. S. Eliot, *Four Quartets*, Faber.

85 Ibsen, *Hedda Gabler*, p. 99.

86 Pinter, *Plays: One*, p. 14.

90 Beckett, *Theatre Annual No. 1*, Calder.

92 Bernard Shaw, *Man and Superman* (1905), Penguin, 1946,
    p. 47.